Marie Curie

Marie
Curie

Vicki Cobb

DK PUBLISHING

LONDON, NEW YORK, MUNICH,
MELBOURNE, AND DELHI

Editor : John Searcy
Publishing Director : Beth Sutinis
Designer : Mark Johnson Davies
Cartographer : Ed Merritt
Art Director : Dirk Kaufman
Photo Research : Anne Burns Images
Production : Ivor Parker
DTP Designer : Kathy Farias

First American Edition, 2008

11 12 10 9 8 7 6 5

012-DD480-August/2008

Published in the United States
by DK Publishing
375 Hudson Street
New York, New York 10014

DK books are available at special discounts
when purchased in bulk for sales
promotions, premiums, fund-raising,
or educational use. For details, contact:

DK Publishing Special Markets
375 Hudson Street
New York, New York 10014
SpecialSales@dk.com

A catalog record for this book is available
from the Library of Congress.

ISBN 978-0-7566-3831-3 (Paperback)
ISBN 978-0-7566-3832-0 (Hardcover)

Printed and bound in China
by South China Printing Co., Ltd.

Photography credits:

Front Cover by Corbis/Bettman
Back Cover by Getty/Popperfoto

Discover more at
www.dk.com

Contents

Prologue

The Joy of Discovery

On a winter evening in 1901, Marie and Pierre Curie were eating dinner in their Paris home with their four-year-old daughter, Irène, and Pierre's father, Dr. Curie, who lived with them. After dinner, Marie put Irène to bed, and Dr. Curie retired to his room. But Pierre was restless. As Marie sat down to her sewing, she sensed his unease and said, "Suppose we go down there for a moment?" Pierre knew exactly where she wished to go: They worked together in a makeshift laboratory, partners in a hunt for something whose existence they believed in but had yet to prove to the world. Every day they put in long hours because they knew they were getting closer and closer to the truth. Their lab was like a magnet that drew them even at the end of a long workday. So they put on their coats and set out, arm in arm, on the five-block stroll to the center of their lives.

Wife, mother, and innovator, Marie Curie was devoted both to her family and to her scientific pursuits.

Marie and Pierre Curie were scientists interested in discovering the basic materials and laws that make up the natural world. By the beginning of

the 20th century, the science of chemistry had determined that all the matter on earth was made of elements—solids, liquids, and gases that could not be simplified. The smallest particle of an element was the atom. Elements could combine with each other to make more complex materials, called compounds. Chemists already knew how to break down compounds to see what elements they were made of. Some of the known elements were gases, like hydrogen, oxygen, and nitrogen; some were metals, like gold, silver, and tin; and some were nonmetals, like carbon and sulfur. By 1898, seventy-nine elements had been discovered.

Recently, Marie Curie had become interested in a new kind of energy that was given off by the element uranium, a rare metal. Uranium emitted rays that were similar to light rays but were invisible to the human eye. They also passed through materials that stopped ordinary light, such as paper or wood. Marie used an instrument invented by her husband to measure the strength of these rays, which she called "radioactivity." When she measured the radioactivity from uranium ore, she discovered that there was far too much radiation to come from uranium alone. Marie guessed that this extra radiation must come from a new and unknown element. She wrote her sister: "You know, Bronya, the radiation that I couldn't explain comes

from a new chemical element. The element is there and I've got to find it. We are sure! The physicists we have spoken to believe we have made an error in experiment and advise us to be careful. But I am convinced that I am not mistaken."

As it turned out, the radiation came from *two* new elements. On that winter evening, the subject of her experiments was the one she called "radium." Marie had set out to find radium in a way that would prove it existed. She would publish her findings so that other scientists could repeat her experiments and get the same results. The job was harder and took longer than she had imagined when she first started. She shared her dreams of the new element with her husband, dreams that fueled her efforts for almost four years of arduous work.

"I wonder what *it* will be like, what *it* will look like. . . . Pierre, what form do you imagine *it* will take?" Marie speculated to her husband.

"I don't know," Pierre answered gently. "I should like it to have a beautiful color."

That night, as they approached the familiar laboratory, they no longer noticed that it was just a wooden shack in a courtyard, that the skylight leaked when it rained, that it was drafty and cold in winter and stifling hot in summer. Pierre put his key in the lock and the door squeaked open. The room was furnished with worn kitchen tables and every surface was covered with tiny glass dishes filled with fluids. The open dishes allowed the fluids to evaporate so that crystals containing their new element would form. "Don't light the lamps," Marie said. "Look . . . look." The dishes glowed in the dark with a strange and beautiful bluish light. These luminous crystals contained the new element, radium. Radium was so rare that it was taking a long time to collect enough of it to measure its properties. Yet its powerful glow was proof that soon they would have enough to do this. At that point, they could publish their results.

Marie's discovery of radium brought her immense joy and satisfaction. It would change the world of medicine and add to our understanding of the structure of the atom. It would bring her fame, though it would not protect her from heartache and disappointment. Marie Curie was a world-class scientist—the first woman to be recognized as such. What did it take for her to become a scientist? What drove her to spend so many of her waking hours in a laboratory, instead of managing her home and family like most women of her day? What was so fascinating about science that it captured her imagination for a lifetime? This book tells the story.

The lab where the Curies discovered radium was less than ideal. A modest stove was the only source of heat.

chapter **1**

A Child of Poland

Marie Curie was the fifth and last child born to Vladislav and Bronislava Sklodowski in Warsaw, Poland, on November 7, 1867. Her name was Marya, but her family called her "Manya," an affectionate nickname, which was customary for all the Sklodowski children. Manya's oldest sister was "Zosia," short for Sophia, next came Joseph or "Jozio," then Bronislava or "Bronya," and finally Helen or "Hela." Both parents were teachers, and their children were all excellent students. Play and education were interchangeable in the Sklodowski household and Manya's special brilliance was evident from early childhood.

When Bronya was eight, she was learning the alphabet using cut-out cardboard letters. She taught her little sister, four-year-old Manya, how to arrange the letters into words. One

Marie Curie was born in this building on Freta Street. The family moved to another section of Warsaw when she was still an infant.

The Sklodowski children (from left to right) were Zosia (11), Hela (5), Manya (4), Jozio (10), and Bronya (8).

morning, Bronya was struggling to read a paragraph during a reading lesson with her parents. Manya grabbed the book and read the opening sentence aloud. Her family reacted with stunned silence, so Manya continued. Suddenly, when she realized that they had made no comment, she burst into tears: "Beg—pardon! Pardon! I didn't do it on purpose. It's not my fault—it's not Bronya's fault! It's only because it was so easy!"

Poor little Manya had misinterpreted her family's reaction and thought she had done something wrong by learning to read on her own. For their part, her parents assured her she

Polish Surnames

When *ski* appears at the end of a Polish surname, it means "son of." The women in families with such names replace *ski* with *ska*, meaning "daughter of."

Manya's mother, Bronislava Boguska, married Vladislav Sklodowski in the summer of 1860.

was not naughty. However, they didn't want to encourage her precocious development; they wanted her to have a normal childhood. So they urged Manya to play or go out into the garden instead of reading books. But Manya's astonishing memory, insatiable curiosity, and intense ability to concentrate wouldn't stay hidden for long.

Manya's parents both came from minor aristocracy—people who once owned land in Poland. Over the past hundred years, invasions by foreign countries had ultimately cost the family its land. Her parents still had money for a good education, however. Her father had studied at the University of Petersburg in Russia and made a living as a teacher of mathematics and science. Her mother was an accomplished pianist and singer and was headmistress of a girls' school in Warsaw. Shortly after Manya was born, Professor Sklodowski moved to a new teaching position at a boys' school in Warsaw, which also provided his family with an apartment. His wife, unfortunately, had to resign her headmistress position because her school was too far away. She now focused her attention on caring for her five children (all born within seven years), supervising their education, and teaching herself how to make shoes for her growing family.

When Manya was five, Mrs. Sklodowska began to feel the debilitating effects of tuberculosis, a slow but deadly disease. To protect her children, she refrained from kissing or hugging them and she kept her eating utensils separate. Manya had to settle for clinging to her mother's skirts and getting a gentle caress on her curly blond hair. She soon learned to control her emotions so that she would not be a burden to her mother.

On Saturday nights, the family would gather around the professor as he read great literature aloud. Manya remembered these evenings as a high point of her childhood. She wrote: "My father . . . even composed poetry himself and was able to translate it from foreign languages into Polish in a very successful way." For Manya, poetry would remain a lifelong love.

Always, there was worry about Mrs. Sklodowska's illness. When Manya was six, her father scraped together enough money to send his wife to a clinic in southern France in the hope of getting her cured. Zosia, then 12, went along to help care for her. They were away for a year. Manya's emotions were tied to reports of her mother's health. When it

Tuberculosis and Typhus

Tuberculosis is a contagious disease in which bacteria cause tiny round lumps to form in the lungs. Symptoms include chest pain, coughing up blood, chills, fever, weight loss, and fatigue. Once a leading cause of death, it can now be prevented by a vaccine and treated with antibiotics. Typhus is a serious disease whose symptoms include a high fever, headaches, and muscle pain. It is caused by germs that live on rats and is spread in areas with poor hygiene.

became clear that the warm climate wasn't helping, Mrs. Sklodowska came home. Unfortunately, her husband lost his job at the boys' school around this time, and the family was forced to move to smaller quarters and take in boarders to help make ends meet.

The crowded living conditions in the Sklodowski household brought a new crisis to the family: typhus. Both Bronya and Zosia came down with this dreaded fever. Zosia never recovered. Her death was a devastating blow to her frail and ailing mother, who lasted another two years and three months before she too was laid to rest at the age of 42.

This map shows the intersection of the three empires that controlled Poland, as they existed in the late 1800s. The modern nation of Poland is shown in orange.

Ríga

Baltic Sea

Gdańsk (Danzig)

Kaliningrad (Konigsberg)

Vilnius

Hamburg

Szczecin

Minsk

Hannover

Berlin

Białystok

Poznań

Szczuki

Warszawa (Warsaw)

GERMAN EMPIRE

Leipzig

Dresden

Łódź

Brest

Wrocław (Breslau)

RUSSIAN EMPIRE

Praha

Katowice

Nürnberg

Kraków

L'viv (Lvov)

Brno

Carpathian Mountains

München

Košice

Salzburg

Wien

Bratislava

AUSTRIA-HUNGARY

Budapest

Debrecen

Botoşani

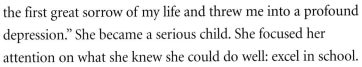

In the early 1860s, there were many protests against the tsar. The prostesters were often subdued with whips.

Manya was nine years old when her mother died. She later said, "This catastrophe was the first great sorrow of my life and threw me into a profound depression." She became a serious child. She focused her attention on what she knew she could do well: excel in school.

There were two kinds of schools in Poland: private Polish schools and public schools run by the government. For the past hundred years, Poland had been partitioned into three sections ruled by three occupying countries: Russia, Austria, and Germany. Several uprisings by the Poles had only tightened the hold of the rulers, especially the Russians, who governed the area containing the city of Warsaw. Their mission was to transform the Poles into loyal Russians by suppressing their language, their religion (which was mostly Catholicism), and their freedom of expression in literature and the press. The many private Polish schools were allowed to continue as long as only Russian was spoken and only Russian-approved content was taught. This policy was enforced by regular school visits from government inspectors.

The Poles, however, found many subtle ways to rebel. This was true even of the schoolchildren. When Manya was 10, she was attending one of these Polish private schools. She was in

15

a class of 25 girls, all dressed in uniforms of navy-blue serge with steel buttons and white, starched collars. Her curly blond hair was pulled back in a single braid. Manya had skipped two grade levels, so she was in the same class as her sister Hela. Their teacher, Miss Tupalska, was a stern-looking woman who was very strict and had high standards for her students. She taught them history and mathematics.

Two of the tsar's Russian soldiers search a Polish civilian, a common scene during Russia's reign.

They had given her the affectionate nickname of "Tupsia."

On this particular day, Tupsia was conducting an act of rebellion: She was teaching a class on Polish history in Polish. Suddenly the lesson was interrupted by an electric bell signal—two long rings followed by two short ones. Four schoolgirls instantly rose and swept up all the books in front of Tupsia and took them into the adjoining dormitory. When Mr. Hornberg, the government school inspector, entered the room the girls were all busy stitching away while Tupsia read aloud to them, in Russian, from a book of Russian fairy tales.

Casually opening a student desk, which was empty, Mr. Hornberg said, "Please call on one of these young people." Manya shrank back in her chair. As the top student in her class, she was always called on to recite, and she hated it!

"Marya Sklodowska," Tupsia said.

Manya stood ready to do her duty for her teacher and classmates.

"Your prayer," commanded Mr. Hornberg.

Manya obediently recited the Lord's Prayer with a flawless Russian accent. What a humiliation for a Polish Catholic schoolgirl, to have to express her religion in a foreign language!

Next he asked her to name all the tsars that had ruled Russia and the names and titles of the current imperial family. There were quite a few names but Manya's excellent memory didn't fail her.

"Who rules over us?"

When Manya didn't respond quickly, Mr. Hornberg repeated the question.

Alexander II of Russia (1818–1881) became tsar in 1855. He was best known for granting the rights of free citizens to Russian peasants, in 1861.

"His Majesty Alexander II, Tsar of All the Russias." Manya's face had a pinched look.

When the session was over and the satisfied Mr. Hornberg finally left, Manya burst into tears as her teacher kissed her on the forehead. If only Mr. Hornberg and other agents of Russian oppression knew how their heavy-handed enforcement backfired. Instead of loyal Russian citizens, they were creating a generation of Polish patriots.

2

Dedicated Students

On June 12, 1883, Manya received the gold medal awarded to the top student in her high school graduating class. She was 15 years old. Gold medals were nothing new to the Sklodowski children. Jozio and Bronya had each received one. The Polish private schools could not legally grant the diploma that was required for admission to universities, so Manya had left the private school after her mother's death to attend the government-run Gymnasium Number Three in downtown Warsaw. It had been a harsh learning environment, compared to the Polish school.

Manya later wrote: "All instruction was given in Russian, by Russian professors, who, being hostile to the Polish nation, treated

This picture was taken shortly before Bronya left for the Sorbonne to study medicine. Manya (left) is 19 and Bronya is 23.

their pupils as enemies . . . "
Even so, she recounted, "I
learned easily mathematics
and physics. . . . I found in
this ready help from my
father, who loved science
and had to teach it himself.
He enjoyed any explanation
he could give us about Nature
and her ways. Unhappily, he had

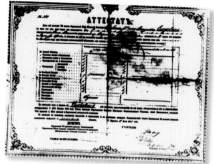

Manya's high-school diploma shows her grades. As an adult, she remembered "always having held first rank in my class."

no laboratory and could not perform experiments." Proud
of her academic accomplishments, Mr. Sklodowski decided
that Manya deserved a year off from school and studying.

Both of Manya's parents came from large families. Many
of her aunts and uncles had homes in the countryside,
where the Sklodowski children usually spent time during
the summers. After graduation, Manya and Hela set off to
spend time at one uncle's home after another, always having
lots of cousins for company. Manya wrote her best friend
Kazia, "I have no schedule. I get up sometimes at ten o'clock,
sometimes at four or five (morning, not evening!) I read no
serious book, only harmless and absurd little novels. . . .

"We go out in a band to walk in the woods. We roll hoops,
we play battledore and shuttlecock (at which I am very bad). . . .
We swing a lot, swinging ourselves hard and high; we bathe,
we go fishing with torches for shrimps . . . Every Sunday the
horses are harnessed for the trip into Mass, and afterward we

Battledore and Shuttlecock

Battledore and shuttlecock is similar to the game of badminton but doesn't use a net. Paddles are used to keep a cork with feathers (the "bird") up in the air. The object of the game is to hit the bird as many times as possible without letting it fall to the ground. In 1830, the record for the number of hits was 2,117, held by an upper class British family.

pay a visit to the vicarage. The two priests are clever and very witty, and we get enormous amusement from their company." Manya became a strong swimmer and a fine horsewoman. She developed a lifelong love of the outdoors.

That winter, Manya and Hela continued their holiday at their father's brother's home in the Carpathian Mountains. Uncle Zdzislav had three daughters and the winter passed quickly with one *kulig* after another. A kulig was a dance party that started out with a horse-drawn sleigh ride. The girls were masked and dressed in the costumes of Polish peasants. Young men on horseback escorted the sleigh, carrying flaming torches. A sleigh of Jewish musicians from the village played the traditional dances—mazurkas, polkas, and waltzes—as other sleighs full of partygoers joined them. They then descended upon a house, whose occupants appeared to have gone to bed, and banged on the door. The master of the house, fully expecting them, welcomed them and the party began in earnest. Food appeared and the dancing began. Then, as if on a signal, the place emptied as the revelers jumped back in the sleighs to go to another house—and then another and another until the sun rose on the exhausted dancers. Manya wrote Kazia, "I have been to a kulig. You can't imagine how delightful it is, especially when the clothes are beautiful and the boys are well dressed . . . There were a great many young men from Cracow, very handsome boys who danced so well! . . . At eight o'clock in the morning we danced the last dance—a white mazurka."

They spent the summer at a luxurious country estate north of Warsaw at the invitation of a former student of their mother's. The girls went swimming and boating by day and went to parties almost every

A cavalcade of sleighs carry merrymakers through the snow-covered countryside of the Carpathian Mountains.

night. Hela later wrote, "The summer passes as quickly as a dream but the memory of it has been lasting. . . . It is good when a person has had at least one such crazy summer in her life."

All good things come to an end. Manya returned to her father's home in September 1884, ready to start thinking seriously about her future. Mr. Sklodowski's greatest disappointment was his inability to pay for the higher education of his four brilliant children. They all wanted a university degree—but they would have to find a way to pay for it. Joseph had won a scholarship to study medicine at the University of Warsaw, so he was well on his way to a career. Hela, the most beautiful of the sisters, had a lovely voice and was receiving free singing lessons. Bronya, like her brother, wanted to be a doctor, but the University of Warsaw was closed to women. Manya wasn't sure what she wanted to do but she knew she wanted to learn more. At the time, there were only three universities in Europe that offered graduate degrees to women. For Manya and Bronya, the Sorbonne in Paris seemed like the best choice. In hope of going there, they decided to earn money by tutoring.

In the meantime, to further their education, Manya and Bronya joined a subversive "Floating University" made up of Polish teachers and intellectuals. It met four nights a week in various attics and cellars around Warsaw and was free to all who attended. There were classes that covered natural history, sociology, and the latest developments in the sciences—physics, chemistry, and physiology. The students were swept up in dreams of freedom for their homeland as they listened to famous lecturers speak about sexual equality, the emancipation of women, and education for all people. They fervently believed that education itself would bring about the political change necessary to return Poland to the Polish people. If the Russian authorities caught wind of the school, both teachers and students could be arrested. Yet the courage and discretion needed to attend only increased the passion of the Polish students, including the Sklodowska sisters. Its purpose was to produce a group of teachers who could enlighten uneducated Poles. Twice a week, Manya volunteered to read aloud to dressmakers while they sewed as a way of helping to educate the masses.

Church spires tower over the old city in Warsaw. Many meetings of the Floating University were held in church basements.

The Sorbonne

Officially, *Collège de Sorbonne* was only the name of the theology school within the University of Paris. However, the word *Sorbonne* was often used to refer to the university as a whole. With origins in the 12th century, the university was one of the most prestigious institutions in the world. It split into 13 independent schools in 1970.

After contributing to household expenses, the girls saved as much as they could from their tutoring income. This was not an especially productive way to realize their dreams. After one year they had saved only enough to pay for a single one-way train trip to Paris and one year's expenses for a five-year course of study. At that rate Bronya would be an old woman before she had a chance to become a doctor. The only solution, as Manya saw it, would be for her to take a live-in job as a governess. There, she would receive room and board and would be able to send most of her pay to Bronya. After Bronya became a doctor, she could then support Manya as she took a turn earning an advanced degree. At first, Bronya protested, but Manya was determined. So in October 1886, the whole family saw Bronya off for the fall term at the Sorbonne, and Manya moved in with a lawyer's family in Warsaw.

This first live-in job proved to be a disaster. Manya found the child to be a spoiled brat, and the mother treated Manya like a servant, when she expected to be treated like one of the family. She lasted only six weeks there. But soon after she returned home, she was offered a three-year contract for another governess job with an excellent salary. The only drawback was that it was in the country, more than 60 miles (97 km) north of Warsaw. Nevertheless, Manya set off on the eight-hour journey to the home of Mr. and Mrs. Zorawski, located on a 200-acre country estate that farmed and processed sugar beets. Manya wrote to her cousin Henrietta about a month after she arrived: "I have seven hours of work a day: four with Andzia and three with Bronka. This is rather a lot, but it doesn't matter. My room is upstairs. It is big, quiet

The Zorawski house in Szczuki, Poland, was Manya's home from 1886 to 1889.

and agreeable. There is a whole collection of children in the Z. family: three sons in Warsaw (one at the university, two in boarding schools). In the house there are Bronka (eighteen years old), Andzia (ten). Stas who is three, and Maryshna, a little girl of six months." She later wrote, "The Z. household is relatively cultivated. Mr. Z. is an old-fashioned man, but full of good sense, sympathetic and reasonable. His wife is rather difficult to live

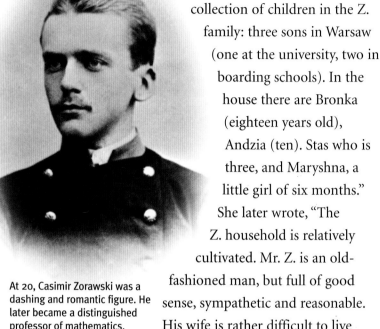

At 20, Casimir Zorawski was a dashing and romantic figure. He later became a distinguished professor of mathematics.

with, but when one knows how to take her she is quite nice. I think she likes me well enough."

As Manya settled in to the Zorawski household, she found time to continue her mission to educate the masses. With the approval of Mrs. Zorawska, she and Bronka gave lessons to 18 village children, to make them literate in their native language. (It was easier to get away with teaching Polish in a rural farming area than it was in a big city with lots of Russian authorities around.) In the evenings, Manya persisted in studying on her own, working toward that far distant dream of attending the Sorbonne. Increasingly, this dream focused on science. She wrote: "These solitary studies were encompassed with difficulty. The scientific education I had received at school was very incomplete—much inferior to the program for the baccalaureate in France. I tried to complete it in my own way, with the help of books got together by sheer chance . . . I acquired a habit of independent work and I learned a certain number of things, which were to be useful to me later." Bronya, for her part, worked hard in Paris, ever grateful for the opportunity given to her by her younger sister. In spite of her homesickness, Manya decided to spend the summer with the Zorawskis so she could continue sending money to Bronya.

Manya was now almost 19. She was quite pretty, with curly blond hair and ash-gray eyes that had an intense, intelligent gaze. She was also quite accomplished. She spoke five languages and could dance, ride a horse, row a boat, compose poetry, and converse knowledgably on a number of subjects. So when the Zorawakis' handsome, 20-year-old son, Casimir, returned on holiday from the university, it was no surprise that he fell madly in love with her. She was so different from the girls he knew in his hometown. Manya, too, was smitten.

First love was a pleasant diversion. Manya's routine existence in this drab, flat countryside stretched endlessly

"I have lost the hope of ever becoming anybody . . ."

—Manya Sklodowska, in a letter to her brother

in front of her as her sister worked towards her medical degree in Paris. No wonder she and Casimir discussed marriage. But Casimir's parents threw a fit when he asked them to approve of their engagement. He was extremely eligible and could easily find a local wife with money. No matter how cultivated Manya was, she was a mere governess and poor. Casimir bowed to his parents' wishes and went back to school in the fall. Nevertheless, some of the romance lingered on through letters and Casimir's occasional visits home.

Manya, crushed with disappointment, stayed on at her post. She needed the job and still had two years to go on her contract. The pay was excellent and she regularly sent money to Bronya. Although she was fulfilling her promise to her sister, she seemed to have lost ambition for herself. She wrote her brother Jozio: "For now that I have lost the hope of ever becoming anybody, all my ambition has been transferred to Bronya and to you. You two, at least must direct your lives according to your gifts." A year later she wrote her cousin Henrietta: "My plans for the future are modest indeed: my dream, for the moment, is to have a corner of my own where I can live with my father. The poor man misses me a lot; he would like to have me at home; he longs for me! . . . Therefore, if the thing is at all possible, I shall leave [here]—which can't be done, in any case, for some time—I shall install myself in

Warsaw, take a post as a teacher in a girls' school and make up the rest of the money I need by giving lessons."

Despite her disappointment in love and the drabness of her existence, Manya soldiered on until her three-year contract had been fulfilled, returning to Warsaw in time for Easter 1889. Her father was now working as the director of a reformatory. It was a thankless job, but the pay was good enough to allow him to contribute support to Bronya every month. Bronya immediately wrote Manya to stop sending her money and to start saving for her own education in Paris. Manya quickly found another position, but this time she signed up for only one year. This new position was quite pleasant. Her new employers were very wealthy and had a home in Warsaw, so she was not cut off from her family. "Mme. F.," her new employer, was very friendly toward the "exquisite" Miss Sklodowska and invited her to tea parties and dances. And although she couldn't see her future clearly, she and her sister were still working their plan.

In 1890, Vladislav Sklodowski poses with his daughters: Manya (left), Bronya, and Hela. This was the last year Manya lived with her father.

chapter **3**

Paris, at Last

In March 1890, a thunderbolt arrived in a letter from Bronya. She was getting married! Her fiancé was Casimir Dluski, a fellow Polish medical student, ten years her senior, who was about to become a doctor. They would be married by the summer. Bronya would have only her final examination before she too would be a doctor. "And now you, my little Manya," Bronya wrote, "you must make something of your life. . . . If you can get together a few hundred rubles this year, you can come to Paris next year and live with us, where you will find board and lodging. It is absolutely necessary to have a few hundred rubles for your fees at the Sorbonne. . . . You must take this decision; you have been waiting too long. I guarantee that in two years you will have your master's degree . . ."

After all this time, however, Manya hesitated. She had promised her father

The Eiffel Tower was a new feature of the Paris skyline when Manya arrived. It had been completed in 1889 for a World's Fair.

that she would come home and
live with him when her current
contract was finished and she
didn't want to break that promise.
She also felt responsible for her
sister Hela, who was the least

> *"You must make something of your life."*
>
> —Bronya Sklodowska, in a letter to Manya

academically gifted of the Sklodowskis. In the background,
there was some unfinished business with Casimir Zorowski,
her old love. She finally decided that this would be her last
live-in governess post. When her contract expired, she would
spend the year with her father, saving money to go to Paris.

During this year at home she busied herself with tutoring,
helping with the plans for her brother Jozio's wedding,
and looking for a position for Hela. She also had access
to a chemistry laboratory, which furthered her interest in
scientific experimentation. By this point, it was becoming
clear to her that this was what she wanted to study. That
summer, Manya met Casimir for the last time. It seemed he
was still dragging his feet about going against his parents
wishes and committing to her. Finally, an exasperated Manya
said to him, "If you can't see a way to clear up our situation,
it is not for me to teach it to you." At long last, Manya had
rediscovered her sense of self-worth and purpose in life. It
was if she had recovered from a long illness. She prepared to
set out for Paris in October 1891.

Manya settled into the second-floor apartment belonging
to Bronya and her husband, an hour's bus ride from the

Sorbonne. At the time of Manya's arrival, the university was undergoing a transformation. New science towers were being built. Science was now in high esteem, attracting both money and outstanding professors to the university. Laboratory research was an essential part of a student's education in the sciences. Imagine Manya's anticipation when she first encountered a white poster announcing: "Faculty of Sciences—First Quarter—Courses will begin at the Sorbonne on November 3, 1891." On her registration card she firmly wrote the French version of her name: "Marie Sklodowska." Now her great strengths—determination, independence, purposefulness, and patience—would be focused on one thing: total immersion in learning science.

During the day, Marie spent all her time at school, returning to the Dluski apartment for dinner and an evening of study. Bronya had created an inviting home, furnished with items brought from Poland and bought at auctions. Among these items was a piano, which her husband played with great enthusiasm. Casimir Dluski was the son of a wealthy Polish family. As a law student in St. Petersburg, he had angered the tsarist police.

The science towers, including one with an observatory, were still being built when Marie entered the Sorbonne.

He had then fled to Paris and switched his focus to medicine. During the day, he and Bronya took turns using one room of their apartment as an office in which to see patients. At other times they were both out making house calls. But the busy evenings at the apartment made it difficult for Marie to study. Almost every night, the Dluskis had company. Polish artists, writers, and musicians dropped by for conversation, music, hot tea, and Bronya's freshly made

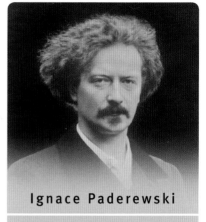

Ignace Paderewski

Ignace Paderewski (1860–1941) was a world-class pianist and composer who amassed a great fortune playing concerts around the world. He was also a devoted Polish patriot. He briefly served as prime minister in 1919 when Poland gained its independence after World War I.

poppy-seed cakes. Always there was talk of freeing Poland. One evening, the famous pianist, Ignace Paderewski, gave an impromptu concert on the Dluskis' modest upright piano. Little did Marie and the Dluskis know that one day Padereweski would be the prime minister of a free Poland.

Marie was challenged by her new environment, and not only because of the difficulty of her studies. Her conversational French needed a great deal of work. There were not many female students in her class, and Marie was

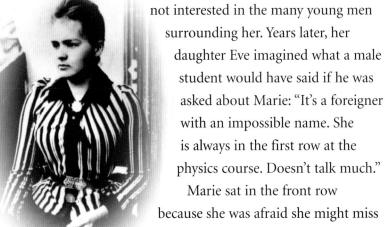

not interested in the many young men surrounding her. Years later, her daughter Eve imagined what a male student would have said if he was asked about Marie: "It's a foreigner with an impossible name. She is always in the first row at the physics course. Doesn't talk much."

Marie sat in the front row because she was afraid she might miss something otherwise. During one lecture, a physics professor said, "I take the sun and I throw it," asking his students to imagine what might happen to all the

This picture was taken on Bronya's balcony just after Marie arrived in Paris. She later gave it to Pierre.

planets under such circumstances. Another professor warned his students, "Don't trust what people teach you, and above all what I teach you." She worked as if in a fever, wishing only that there were no distractions. By March, she knew she had to make a change. The two-hour round-trip bus rides to school and the evening activities at the Dluskis were interfering with her work. Reluctantly, her sister and brother-in-law helped her move to a drafty attic room a block from the Sorbonne.

As inexpensive as her new lodgings were, living independently put an extra burden on Marie's overstretched finances. But she didn't care. She simply cut down on food to make ends meet. One day that spring, Casimir received word

34

from some friends that Marie had fainted on the sidewalk. He and Bronya decided she was undernourished and brought her home for a few days to feed her. Later, Casimir would call her student days "my sister-in-law's heroic period." Marie didn't even take the summer off. She used it to perfect her French and take extra math courses. A year later, in 1893, she received her master's degree in physics, graduating at the top of her class. In 1894, she received a second master's degree in mathematics, graduating second in her class. She later wrote, "I shall always consider one of the best memories of my life that period of solitary years exclusively devoted to the studies, finally within my reach, for which I had waited so long."

These trams on the Boulevard de Strasbourg are typical of the kind Marie used to commute to school.

chapter 4

Science at the End of the 19th Century

What was it about science that grabbed the imaginations of so many? It is only natural for human beings to try and make sense about the planet we live on. Yet nature is complicated and bewildering—a puzzle that seems beyond human comprehension. How does one eat such an elephant? The answer: one bite at a time. Science began by chopping up the enormous subject of the natural world into smaller, more manageable questions that could be answered by conducting experiments.

In addition to his work on heat theory, Count Rumford invented central heating, a smokeless chimney, a kitchen oven, and a pressure cooker.

What is the world made of? Energy and matter. With some overlap, the study of energy became the subject of physics, and the study of matter became the subject of chemistry. Definitions in science are very precise. Energy is defined as the ability to do work. Work is defined as the

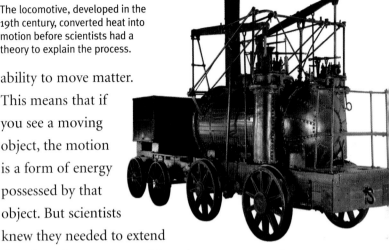
The locomotive, developed in the 19th century, converted heat into motion before scientists had a theory to explain the process.

ability to move matter. This means that if you see a moving object, the motion is a form of energy possessed by that object. But scientists knew they needed to extend the idea of energy beyond just the movement of matter.

In 1776, when the American colonies declared their independence, an American scientist named Benjamin Thompson moved to England because of his loyalty to the British crown. He later became a public servant in Germany, where he was rewarded with the title of Count Rumford. At the time, it was believed that heat was a kind of matter called caloric fluid. Hot materials were thought to have more caloric fluid than colder ones. If so, caloric fluid should weigh something. In the 1780s, Count Rumford decided to see if he could detect caloric fluid by conducting extensive experiments weighing all kinds of hot and cold objects. He compared the weight of water when it was frozen to its weight after it melted. There was no difference in the weight, although the prevailing theory predicted that water would gain weight as it melted. After years of experiments trying to determine the weight of

Perpetual Motion Machines

Inventors have long dreamed of creating a perpetual-motion machine, which would run forever without the help of any external source of energy. We now know that it's impossible. Friction, in which one moving surface touches another, generates heat. This heat is lost to the machine and is no longer available to do work, so the machine will ultimately run down and stop. It is impossible to design a machine without some friction.

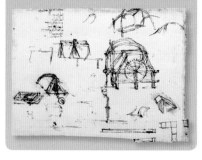

heat, Rumford concluded that "all attempts to discover any effect of heat upon the apparent weight of bodies will be fruitless." His experiments had only produced a dead end.

Then, one day, Count Rumford was in an arsenal watching workers drill a bore in what would become a brass cannon. He noticed that as they rotated the drill bit, both the barrel of the cannon and the metal chips got very hot. He correctly concluded that the source of all that heat was the motion of the drill against the brass and, as long as the drill kept spinning, the supply of heat was inexhaustible. Aha! There was a connection between motion and heat. A British scientist named James Prescott Joule read about Rumford's discovery and made accurate measurements of motion and the heat it produced. Joule discovered that every bit of heat and motion could be accounted for.

It turned out that there were many other cases where one kind of energy became another. Sound could produce motion. Heat could produce light. Electricity, potentially the most useful form of energy, could produce motion, heat, light, and sound. Accurate measurements of how much of one type of energy was needed to produce another type was leading to an extraordinary idea about energy, known as the Law of Conservation of Energy. This law states that energy can be neither created nor destroyed; it can only be transformed from one kind to another.

The study of matter, the "stuff" the earth is made of, began in medieval times through the work of people called alchemists, who were pursuing a get-rich-quick scheme: making gold from less valuable metals. The alchemists never found a way to make gold, but they did develop a number of techniques for purifying chemicals and combining them to make new materials—techniques that chemists would use later on. By the beginning of the 19th century, it was clear that there were a number of substances that could not be separated into two or more other substances. These were called elements.

Some of these pieces of 14th-century alchemist's equipment might be found in a modern chemistry lab.

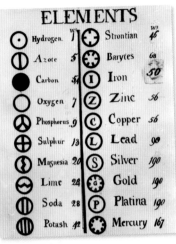

ELEMENTS

		w^t			w^t
⊙	Hydrogen	1	✛	Strontian	46
◐	Azote	5	✳	Barytes	68
●	Carbon	54	①	Iron	50
○	Oxygen	7	Ⓩ	Zinc	56
✪	Phosphorus	9	Ⓒ	Copper	56
⊕	Sulphur	13	Ⓛ	Lead	90
◑	Magnesia	20	Ⓢ	Silver	190
⊖	Lime	24	✿	Gold	190
◍	Soda	28	Ⓟ	Platina	190
◍	Potash	42	✺	Mercury	167

John Dalton knew of 36 elements when he developed this table, which was a precursor to our modern periodic table.

In 1810, Englishman John Dalton put forth the theory that all matter is made up of tiny, indivisible particles called atoms. According to this theory, each element has its own kind of atom, and there are as many different kinds of atoms as there are elements. Different elements combine to make other forms of matter called compounds. The smallest part of a compound consists of a group of a definite number of atoms. Dalton called this group "compound atoms." We call them molecules. Finally, he figured out that in chemical reactions, atoms are neither created nor destroyed, but only rearranged. This was the first statement of a law that became known as the Law of Conservation of Matter. No one had ever seen an atom, but the idea of the atom was useful because it explained what happened in chemical reactions.

Measurement, so important in physics, was equally important in chemistry. Frenchman Joseph Louis Gay-Lussac made some amazing discoveries when he began measuring the volumes of gaseous elements and the gaseous compounds they formed together. In one experiment, he found that two volumes of hydrogen and one volume of oxygen react explosively to form two volumes of water vapor, or steam.

The simplicity of his results was astounding! Under equal pressure and temperature, volumes of gas always combined in predictable ways. Eventually, he came to suspect that these results might be related to the composition of molecules. For example, he concluded that a molecule of water was made up of two atoms of hydrogen (H) and one of oxygen (O). The chemical formula for water is now written as H_2O.

In the early part of the 19th century, there were only four known elements that were gases: nitrogen, oxygen, hydrogen, and chlorine. Hydrogen was the lightest element, so chemists gave it an atomic weight of one. The weights of all other elements could now be compared to hydrogen. An equal volume of oxygen weighed 16 times the weight of hydrogen, so it was given the atomic weight of 16. Nitrogen was 14. Little by little, with hundreds of scientists working away in their individual labs, publishing their results and reading each other's work, the atomic weights of all the known

Joseph Gay-Lussac is honored as a "hero of work" in this French trading card.

elements were determined. Each element had its own atomic weight.

The atomic weight was only one of many properties that described each element. Elements could also be classified according to whether they were a metal or a nonmetal; a solid, liquid, or gas at room temperature; and the temperatures at which they changed from a liquid to a gas (the boiling point) or from a liquid to a solid (the freezing point).

Found in most sand and clay, silicon is the second most abundant element on earth after oxygen.

Although most elements were solids, there were several gases and two liquids (bromine and mercury). The amount of each element on earth also differed enormously. Some, like silicon or nitrogen, were very abundant, while others were quite rare. Was there any way to organize the elements into some kind of system? That puzzle looked like a tough nut to crack.

One place to start looking was the chemical properties of elements—the ways they reacted with other elements to form compounds. A certain group of elements (fluorine, chlorine, bromine, and iodine) reacted violently with a group of metals (lithium, sodium, and potassium) to form stable white crystals known as salts. The formulas for all these salts had the same form: one atom of each element. Common table salt contains one atom of sodium and one atom of chlorine. Chemists had identified other groups of elements based on the ways they formed compounds. One group acted like nitrogen, another like oxygen.

Russian chemist Dmitri Mendeleev made an interesting observation. He started arranging the elements in a row from left to right, in order of increasing atomic weight. He started with lithium and placed heavier elements next to it until he came to the seventh element, fluorine. The element after fluorine was sodium. Since sodium behaved exactly like lithium chemically, Mendeleev started a new row and put sodium directly under lithium. The seventh element of the second row turned out to be chlorine, which behaved just like fluorine, which was directly above it. After chlorine, Mendeleev started a third row with the metal potassium, which behaved just like the other two elements above it. Each column formed a family of elements. It was like a librarian was putting books on a shelf from left to right in order of increasing number of pages. The first book might be poetry; the second, history; the third, geography; and so on. When he started the next shelf, he found the subject of each book was the same as the

Demitri Mendeleev was the youngest of 15 children. His mother operated a glassworks.

THE
MAGAZINE OF SCIENCE,
And School of Arts.

No. IV.]   SATURDAY, APRIL 27, 1829.   [Price 1½d.

FAC-SIMILES OF PHOTOGENIC DRAWINGS.

Magazines promoting scientific ideas to the general public became increasingly popular in the 19th century.

one directly above it. There seemed to be no connection between number of pages and the subject, but the orderliness was amazing.

Mendeleev formulated a law to describe his astonishing discovery: When elements are put in order of increasing atomic weight, there is a periodic repetition of chemical properties. Mendeleev had no idea why this was so, but it was a very useful rule because every once in a while, there was a gap in the table. Some element was obviously missing. Chemists now knew they had to look for the unknown element. But it wasn't a blind search. It would have an atomic weight between those of its two neighbors in the row and it would behave like the family members above it.

When Marie Sklodowska arrived at the Sorbonne, there were 79 known chemical elements. The Law of Conservation of Energy was firmly established. Science was like a huge international game whose goal was to discover the laws that explained nature, and it was riveting to its participants. It involved cooperation between scientists as they shared their discoveries through meetings and the publication of their works. But the game of science was also highly competitive.

The Periodic Table

Mendeleev's table is now known as the periodic table of the elements. It lists every known element in order. These include 92 naturally occurring elements, as well as many more that have been artificially created by scientists. The 57th spot on the table is taken up by 15 elements, all very much alike, called the "rare earth" elements. Another set of 15 elements occupies the 89th place. (The two rows at the bottom represent these sets.) Today, the periodic table is an essential component of every chemistry classroom.

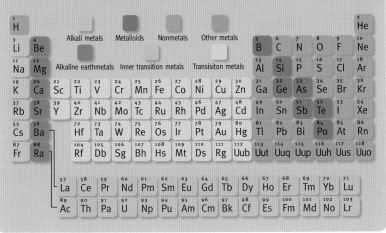

Since there was only one nature to be discovered, the scientist who published first was usually given credit for a discovery. Doubtless every discovery, no matter how small, gave some measure of satisfaction to the "player." But a big discovery, one that opened up a new world of investigation, was a guarantee of immortality. As a student, Marie Sklodowska was certain of one thing: When it came to science, she wanted to be a player.

chapter 5

Pierre

The body of work that we call science accumulates from the contributions of many people over the years. To enter the game of science, Marie had to catch up to where science was at the end of the 19th century. She had to learn advanced mathematics, the language of science.

An electroscope is one of the many instruments Marie had to become familiar with in order to work in a laboratory.

She had to learn the established laws of physics and chemistry. She had to learn how to work in a laboratory, which involved techniques of measurement and the use of scientific instruments. Marie had started studying at the Sorbonne just before she turned 24. She had family obligations in Paris to Bronya and her husband. Although she had won a scholarship, which was paying for her second year of study, she was still restricted by lack of money. She had been unlucky in love. She was also committed to her father and her homeland, and was preparing to return to her beloved Poland, where she would teach future generations. In spite of the

This engraving depicts a physics research laboratory at the Sorbonne. It is likely Marie visited this very lab.

fact that she was a lovely young woman surrounded by young men, she had no interest or time in her life for romance.

In the winter of 1894, a young Polish physics professor named Joseph Kovalski was visiting Paris with wife, who had been a friend of Marie's when she worked for the Zorawskis. He was on his honeymoon, but he was also giving a few lectures at the Physics Society, which Marie attended. In a conversation after a lecture, Marie told him that she had been given a job studying the magnetic properties of steel. The research involved some large equipment, too large for the crowded student lab available to her. She needed more space to do her experiments—did he know of any available?

"I have an idea," Joseph Kovalski said to her after a moment of reflection. "I know a scientist of great merit who works in the School of Industrial Physics and Chemistry in the Rue Lhomond. Perhaps he might have a workroom available. In any case he could give you some advice. Come and have tea tomorrow evening, after dinner, with my wife and me. I will ask the young man to come.

You probably know his name: it is Pierre Curie."

The next evening would change Marie's life in a completely unexpected way. Her laboratory-space problem would not be solved immediately, but she met the man who would become her husband. Marie later described her first impression of Pierre: "He seemed to me very young, though he was at that time thirty-five years old. I was struck by the

Pierre Curie was a careful thinker. He was willing to spend time and effort to fully understand things others dismissed casually.

open expression of his face and by the slight suggestion of detachment in his whole attitude. His speech, rather slow and deliberate, his simplicity, and his smile, at once grave and youthful, inspired confidence."

Pierre Curie did not know how to flirt or make small talk. "We began a conversation," Marie later wrote, "which soon became friendly. It first concerned certain scientific matters about which I was very glad to be able to ask his opinion. Then we discussed certain social and humanitarian subjects which interested us both. There was, between his conceptions and mine, despite the difference between our native countries, a surprising kinship, no doubt attributable to a certain likeness in the moral atmosphere in which we were both raised."

Long ago, Pierre Curie had experienced an early and unhappy love affair that made him swear off women as a distraction from his work as a scientist. He firmly believed that "[A] woman loves life for the living of it far more than we do: women of genius are rare." Imagine his astonishment at meeting an attractive female who spoke to him as an equal in mathematics and physics! It turned out that in spite of the difference in their nationalities, Marie and Pierre did indeed have a great deal in common. Both came from families that had more education than money. (Pierre's father was a doctor.) Both had been educated by their parents. (Pierre had been home-schooled until a tutor discovered his remarkable mind at the age of 14.) Both of them had fathers who loved science and passed this love on to them. Their fathers also had a belief in freedom that went against their respective governments, and

Marie was intrigued by Pierre's ideas, and the way he expressed himself, rather than by any superficial charms.

Pierre leans on his brother, Jacques, in this family portrait. His mother sews while Dr. Curie enjoys his garden.

each had paid a price professionally for his political beliefs. At the end of that first evening, a smitten Pierre asked to see Marie again.

At the time of their meeting, Pierre Curie was recognized as a scientific genius abroad, due to his scientific publications, but was almost unknown in his own country. He had no personal ambition for himself—he only wished to contribute to the body of scientific knowledge. As a result, after 15 years of work, he was teaching at the School of Industrial Physics and Chemistry, an institution much less esteemed than the Sorbonne. His salary was about the same as a specialized worker in a factory. He had not yet acquired his doctorate degree, an essential requirement for teaching at the highest levels of the university. When he was offered the opportunity to compete for a position, he refused, finding the process distasteful. For the most part, he refused to accept medals and honors for his work.

He was an idealist and a dreamer, with little thought for the practicalities entailed by marriage. But when Marie entered his life, things began to change.

The friendship deepened over the spring. Marie was studying for her examination in mathematics, and Pierre was very supportive, hoping that she would graduate at the top of her class. (She eventually came in second.) Pierre believed that science had the potential to save the world and that there was nothing nobler than dedicating one's life to it. He wanted Marie to share his dream. And, although he had a hard time coming out and saying it, that meant he wanted her to share his life. But Marie, in her independent way, nevertheless returned to Poland for her summer vacation. Pierre pursued her in his letters. "It would be a beautiful thing, in which I hardly dare hope, to pass through life together hypnotized in our dreams: your dream for your country, our dream for humanity; our dream for science. Of all these dreams, I believe the last, alone, is legitimate. I mean to say by this that we are powerless to change the social order. Even if this were not true, we shouldn't

Piezoelectricity

In 1880, Pierre Curie and his brother Jacques discovered that when a certain kind of crystal was squeezed, an electric charge built up on its surface. This effect, known as piezoelectricity, gave scientists a way to measure very small electric charges. Its first practical use was in World War I, when it was used to detect underwater submarines.

> *"It seemed to me that the little room that day sheltered the exaltation of human thought."*
>
> —Marie Curie, in her autobiography

know what to do. . . . From the scientific point of view, on the contrary, we can hope to accomplish something; the territory here is more solid and every discovery, no matter how small, lives on."

Pierre's only sibling was his older brother, Jacques, who was also a scientist. They had worked together for years quite fruitfully. Then Jacques had married and moved away, and Pierre missed him greatly, particularly in the lab. Did he see the possibility of a new lab partner in Marie? He later said that he had no doubt that he wanted more than that from Marie. He wanted her to be his wife. Even so, he couldn't quite come out and propose marriage. He could only hope she would return to Paris in October to continue her studies. Marie's small bit of encouragement was to send him a photo of herself, which Pierre affectionately called the "good little student."

Pierre wrote back, "I showed your photograph to my brother. Was that wrong? He admired it. He added: 'She has a very decided look, not to say stubborn.'"

When Marie returned, she thought it would be her final year in Paris. She was still determined to return to Poland and live with her father. Pierre became terrified that he would lose her. He suggested that she share an apartment with him that was divided into two separate units. Marie said no. Four years earlier, Pierre had begun some very original work studying the effect of heat on magnetic materials, but he hadn't gotten around to presenting his thesis to his professors at the Sorbonne, the final step for earning a doctorate. Now, to show Marie that he was serious about their future life together, he finally set the presentation date for March. He invited Marie to attend. When Pierre spoke about science, he was articulate and powerful—absolutely mesmerizing.

This was so different from the way he spoke to Marie about his feelings for her. She wrote, "I have a very vivid memory of how he sustained his thesis before the examiners. . . . I remember the simplicity and clarity of the exposition, the esteem indicated by the attitude of the professors. . . . I was greatly impressed: it seemed to me that the little room that day sheltered the exaltation of human thought." For Marie, Pierre at his best was dazzling.

Shortly before her wedding, Marie poses in a typical dress of the Victorian era, with draped sleeves, a tiny waist, and a flared skirt.

Marie's family had met Pierre's parents at the beginning of the year. Pierre's mother had taken Bronya aside and said, "There isn't a soul on earth to equal my Pierre. Don't let your sister hesitate. She will be happier with him than with anybody." But stubborn Marie did hesitate for most of the school year. Finally, as an act of desperation, Pierre offered to move to Poland, if only she would marry him. He could teach French there and do experiments on the side.

How could she resist this offer? After almost a year of gentle persuasion, Marie, at long last, agreed to marry Pierre. She would become a French citizen and continue to study and teach in France, but she and Pierre would visit Poland the following year. They got married with no great fuss on July 26, 1895. Bronya's mother-in-law offered to make her wedding dress. But Marie didn't want a dress— she wanted a simple suit. Marie told her, "If you are going to be kind enough to give me one, please let it be practical and dark, so that I can put it on afterwards to go to the laboratory." On their wedding day she dressed in a navy-blue woolen suit and a blue blouse with lighter blue stripes. Pierre picked her up in Paris and they took a train to Sceaux, where his parents

Marie and Pierre cycled through these rolling hills of Gascony on their "wedding tramp."

Pierre and Marie are shown about to leave on their honeymoon with their new "safety" bicycles, which were relatively modern for the time.

lived. They were married by a judge at the city hall and returned for an afternoon party at Pierre's parents' home. The guests included Casimir and Bronya and some friends from the university. Marie's father and her sister, Hela, had come from Poland. The newlyweds left the party on their new bicycles, a wedding gift, to spend their honeymoon roaming the French countryside. The only outward signs of celebration were the flowers on Marie's handlebars.

The Search for a Search

After an idyllic summer on their "wedding tramp," Marie and Pierre settled into a fourth-floor, three-room apartment with a view of a garden. The living room served as their office, furnished with only a table and two chairs. Housekeeping was not high on Marie's agenda, and the couple had no intention of entertaining others. So they refused all furniture from Pierre's parents to keep things as simple and easy to care for as possible. Cooking was enough of a challenge for the student-bride. Marie described their life in a letter she wrote to her brother Joseph that November:

> Everything goes well with us; we are both healthy and life is kind to us. I am arranging my

This is Marie and Pierre Curie's wedding photograph, taken in 1895. She did not wear traditional bridal attire.

flat little by little, but I intend to keep it to a style which will give me no worries and will not require attention, as I have very little help: a woman who comes

for an hour a day to wash dishes and do the heavy work. I do the cooking and housekeeping myself.

Every few days we go to Sceaux to see my husband's parents. This does not interrupt our work; we have two rooms on the first floor there with everything we need; we are therefore perfectly at home and can do all the part of our work that cannot be done in the laboratory.

My 'lucrative' employment is not yet settled. I hope to get some work this year that I can do in the laboratory. It is half-scientific, half-industrial occupation, which I prefer to giving lessons.

Pierre earned a small teacher's salary at the School of Physics. Marie was studying for a fellowship competition. If she got the highest grade, she would be awarded a paid teaching position. Space was found in Pierre's laboratory to finish her work on the magnetic properties of steel. In her precise, scientific handwriting, Marie kept a ledger of all their expenses and made notes on her culinary successes and failures. The following summer, she passed her fellowship examination first in her class, so she was now certified to teach high-school physics. She was also expecting their first child. Irène Curie was

born on September 12, 1897. Marie was a devoted mother and kept accurate records of every delightful step of Irène's development. Running a household that now contained a baby while continuing her studies was extremely stressful for the young mother. Fortunately, help came from Pierre's father. Pierre's mother had died a month after Irène was born. Now bereaved and lonely, Dr. Curie offered to come live with his son's family and help out. The offer was quickly accepted. Thus, with the blessings of her husband and father-in-law, Marie pressed on to the next step in her career—earning a doctorate from the Sorbonne.

The main requirement for this highest of all academic degrees is original research. Marie had to decide what she wished to spend her time and energies investigating. There is always a lot of work to do in science. In the wake of breakthrough discoveries, there are plenty of blanks for scientists to fill in. In the 1890s, for example, chemists could do research to fill in the missing elements in the periodic table. This was the safe path. A riskier choice was to research something new and unknown, the path less traveled. Such research could turn out to be extremely fruitful—it might lead to a brand-new breakthrough—or it could be a dead end, wasting months, if not years, of work. Marie began her search for a research project by looking into some of the most interesting recent discoveries.

By the middle of the 19th century, experiments with electricity were quite advanced. For example, when a metal sphere with a negative electric charge is brought near a metal sphere with a positive charge, a huge spark crackles and jumps between the spheres, just like lightning. In 1875, British scientist Sir William Crookes wondered what would happen if you removed the air around the spark. He put electrodes at each end of a glass tube and pumped out the air. When he turned on the current, the yellow, crackling spark had changed into a quiet green glow traveling from the cathode (the negative pole) to the anode (the positive pole). He called the ray a "cathode ray." Cathode rays were a subject of great fascination.

This caricature of Sir William Crookes shows him holding one of his famous cathode-ray tubes.

On November 8, 1895, German scientist Wilhelm Roentgen was doing experiments with a Crookes cathode-ray tube. He had also been studying fluorescent materials— chemicals that glowed when light hit

ELECTRODE

An electrode is a piece of metal that can conduct electricity.

When asked about the moment when he discovered X-rays, Roentgen said, "I didn't think; I investigated."

them. He noticed that a nearby screen painted with fluorescent materials glowed when the cathode-ray tube was on. He wondered if the light from the Crookes tube caused the fluorescence. So he covered the tube with black cardboard and pulled down the shades to see if any light escaped from the tube. Even when the tube was completely covered, the screen glowed. He moved the screen farther away and turned it away from the tube. Still it glowed. He placed his hand between the tube and the screen. Astonishment! There on the screen was the silhouette of the bones inside his hand. These mysterious, invisible rays went through the cardboard around the tube and his flesh. Only his bones cast a shadow! Roentgen gave the name "X-rays" to this unknown, penetrating light. Like visible light, X-rays could expose photographic plates, so Roentgen was able to make permanent records of their amazing powers. One of his most famous pictures was of the skeleton of his wife's hand, clearly showing the ring on her finger.

X-rays were something completely new—invisible light that could penetrate all kinds of solid materials that blocked ordinary light: tin, paper, rubber, even wood. Only very heavy metals such as lead stopped its path. The publication of Roentgen's work at the end of 1895 caused a sensation around the world.

Three weeks later, a Frenchman named Henri Becquerel, whose father and grandfather had been scientists, attended a lecture on X-rays at the French Academy of Sciences. The lecture included a discussion of phosphorescence—a phenomenon in which a material retains a glow after it has been exposed to visible light. This interested Becquerel because his father had done research on the subject. He decided to see if phosphorescent materials gave off X-rays. He had some

This X-ray picture of Roentgen's wife's hand was famous throughout the scientific community, but it made Mrs. Roentgen feel uneasy.

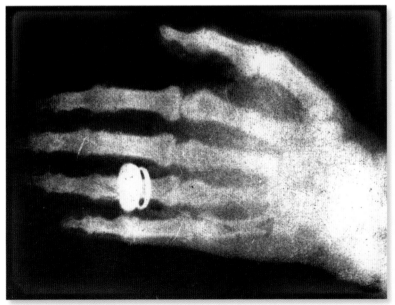

Boequerel

As the son and grandson of prominent French scientists, Henri Becquerel was considered scientific "royalty."

phosphorescent rocks containing uranium minerals, which glowed after being exposed to sunlight. He put the rocks in the sun and then, while they were still glowing, put them on top of photographic plates that had been wrapped in black paper to block the light. When he developed the plates, he found that they had been exposed in the area under the rock. This meant that some rays had passed from the rock through the lightproof paper. Next he wanted to see if the rays could pass through copper. So he put a copper cross on top of a wrapped photographic plate. But when he was about to put his phosphorescent rock in the sun to "excite" it, he found that it had started to rain. So he put the rock on top of the cross and placed everything in a drawer to wait for a sunny day.

It rained for several days. Frustrated with the weather, Becquerel decided not to wait for the sun but to develop the plate that had been sitting in the drawer. To his great surprise, it was more exposed than the ones made from

Uranium

A silvery white metal in its pure state, uranium is the heaviest element found in nature. In the 19th century, it was used for making beautiful yellow glass. It was first isolated in 1841.

rocks that had been exposed to sunlight! The shadow of the cross could clearly be seen in the center of the exposed area. The rays had nothing to do with excitement from the sun. They had nothing to do with a cathode-ray tube. They were different from anything anyone had ever come across.

Becquerel continued his experiments, investigating the source and nature of the rays. He found that all minerals that contained uranium gave off these mysterious rays, even those that were not phosphorescent. Pure uranium metal was the most active. The rays were emitted steadily, without losing strength, and would continue for years. He found that the rays penetrated thin metallic screens and that they acted like light— they could be reflected off a mirror and bent through a prism. Unlike light, they also gave off a weak electric current. He know this because they could be bent with a magnet, like cathode rays. Becquerel wrote six papers on his mysterious rays in 1897. Then, believing the subject had been "squeezed dry," he lost interest and moved on to other things.

One thing Becquerel had not done was measure the strength of the rays. The exposure on the plate was fuzzy, and the intensity of the

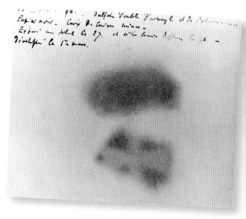

A page from Becquerel's notebook shows the exposure left by uranium salts. The shadow of the cross is visible at the bottom.

exposure depended on how long the rock sat on the plate. It was not an exact measurement. Marie wondered if there was another way to measure the strength of the rays? Why not use the weak electric current in the air that was associated with the rays? The rays caused air molecules to turn into electrically charged particles called ions, which could conduct electricity. The challenge was finding a way to measure this tiny amount of electricity accurately. Pierre Curie just happened to have invented such an instrument.

Pierre and his brother Jacques had developed a device known as a piezoelectrc scale. At the top of the scale was a quartz crystal, which emitted a tiny electric current when it was squeezed. As the pressure on the crystal increased, so did its electrical output. The scale used a series of weights to apply a precise amount of pressure to the crystal, creating a known amount of electric charge. Using some additional components, this charge could be compared to the charge produced by a uranium sample, contained in a nearby chamber. When the two charges were equal, Marie would have an accurate measurement of

Pierre's instrument measures the electricity generated by the crystal at the top in response to weights placed on the tray below.

Marie operates the piezoelectric scale in the lab as Pierre looks on. As can be seen, she is intently focused on the task.

the electricity produced by the uranium.

Marie began her research by mastering Pierre's scale and making sure that it did indeed measure the strength of the mysterious rays. Becquerel had tried to use the instrument but had given up because it was too delicate. It took Marie three weeks to learn how to use it. This was no easy task. Even a fingerprint could change the reading, so the weights had to be placed very carefully on the little tray. She had to sit ramrod straight, with her eyes focused on a glass plate, where a spot of light shifted position based on how much the charge produced by the weights differed from the charge produced by her specimen. With her right hand, she placed the weights on the scale, one by one, without looking at what her hand was doing, similar to a pianist reading music.

She did this until the spot of light stayed in the center of the plate, indicating that the charges were equal. Since the charge from the uranium built up over the course of the session, time was also involved in her measurements. In her left hand she held a stopwatch to keep track of it. All this required intense concentration and dexterity. Perhaps no other scientist could have done as well. Finally, Marie was ready to start investigating.

Nature Doesn't Lie

Marie began her studies by measuring the "Becquerel rays" that were emitted by all the known compounds of uranium. Another element, thorium, had also been shown to emit radiation, so she looked at thorium compounds as well. She reported: "I have investigated . . . the compounds of thorium and uranium and have taken a great many measurements of their activity under different conditions. The result of all these determinations . . . seems to depend upon the presence of the atoms of the two elements . . . and is not influenced by any change of the physical state or chemical decomposition." In other words, the rays were a property of the atoms of uranium and thorium. She called this property "radioactivity." This conclusion—that radioactivity was a unique

Marie rinses crystals in a tiny evaporating dish. The Curies used hundreds of these dishes to isolate radium.

Uranium ore is known as pitchblende due to its black color. The print shows pitchblende miners in England.

WILLS'S CIGARETTES.

MINING PITCHBLENDE

property of atoms—
was Marie Curie's great insight.

The next obvious question was: Do other elements have the property of radioactivity? Marie obtained all kinds of minerals from colleagues and tested them in her apparatus. She found that only minerals containing uranium or thorium were radioactive. This was as she expected. But then she got some surprising results. She was conducting tests on uranium ore (the naturally occurring rock from which uranium is extracted), also known as pitchblende. She knew how much uranium was in the pitchblende, and how much radioactivity that amount of uranium was capable of producing. But the radioactivity emitted by the pitchblende was four times that amount! What could be causing this extra activity? Chemists had analyzed pitchblende extensively. Marie could account for 99 percent of the minerals found in it. If there was another radioactive substance in pitchblende, it had to be in that tiny one percent, and it had to be extremely radioactive if such a tiny amount gave off so much radiation.

Marie repeated her measurements over and over again. She discussed her results with Pierre. They both knew that nature

Vaseline Glass

In nature, certain uranium minerals have a brilliant yellow-green color that was used to create "vaseline" glass, which was popular in the 19th century. Today, vaseline glass is a valuable collectible. It is slightly radioactive but has been declared safe for household use.

doesn't lie. There must be some unknown element in the pitchblende that they could isolate by ordinary chemical means. The problem was so interesting that Pierre quit his own research on crystals to help his wife look for the unknown element.

Pierre's help was very welcome, since there were a number of obstacles to overcome. First, they needed to obtain a large amount of pitchblende—at least a ton—to start with. Pitchblende was expensive because of its commercial value; uranium minerals gave glass a beautiful yellow-green color. Perhaps they could obtain pitchblende residue that was left over after the uranium had been removed? As it happened, the Austrian government owned a uranium mine, and agreed to give the Curies a ton of highly radioactive residue that had been discarded.

Another problem was finding a place to work. Pierre asked the director of the School of Physics if the school had a spare workroom. Marie described the place the school gave them as "an abandoned shed, which had been in service as a dissecting room of the School of Medicine. Its glass roof did not afford complete shelter against rain; the heat was suffocating in summer and the bitter cold of winter was only a little lessened by the iron stove . . . There was no question of obtaining the needed proper apparatus in common use by chemists. We simply had some old pine-wood tables with furnaces and gas burners. We had to use the adjoining yard for those of our chemical operations that involved producing irritating gases;

"It was in this miserable old shed that we passed the best and happiest years of our life . . ."

—Marie Curie, in her autobiography

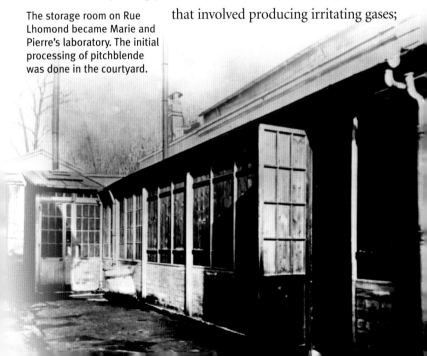

The storage room on Rue Lhomond became Marie and Pierre's laboratory. The initial processing of pitchblende was done in the courtyard.

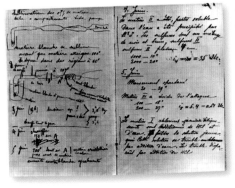

This page from the Curies' notebook shows Pierre's notes on the lefthand page and Marie's on the right.

even then, the gas often filled our shed. With this equipment we entered on our exhausting work.

"Yet it was in this miserable old shed that we passed the best and happiest years of our life, devoting our entire days to our work."

In the beginning, the work was backbreaking. Forty-pound batches of residue had to be boiled with a strong alkali. The residue then had to be subjected to a series of chemical treatments. After each treatment, Marie tested all of the resulting substances for radioactivity, then continued to work on the radioactive portion. Each step further refined the radioactive component. The Curies found that, at a certain point, two different batches were radioactive. One batch was associated with the element bismuth, the other with the element barium. Neither bismuth nor barium was itself radioactive, so Marie figured that there must be two previously undiscovered radioactive elements hiding in these two batches.

Marie was in a hurry to let the world know of her discovery of new radioactive elements. She wrote a paper discussing her early measurements, the atomic property of radioactivity, and the evidence of

ALKALI

An alkali is a solution that reacts strongly with acids to form salts and water.

new elements that were more radioactive than uranium. In the spring of 1898, this paper was presented at the Academy of Sciences by her professor. It didn't get much notice from the international scientific community. Marie had yet to prove the existence of these new elements by the higher standards used by chemists. To do this, she had to find their unique light patterns and their atomic weights.

Every element can be heated to the point that it glows. The light a glowing element gives off can be analyzed by passing it through a prism, producing a distinctive spectrum of bright lines. The instrument that analyzes the spectrum of elements is called a spectroscope. Each element gives off its own unique line pattern, which is like a fingerprint for that element. (Sodium, for example, produces a bright yellow line.) The Curies had a colleague named Eugène Demarçay who worked nearby and was an expert in these matters. Despite the fact that he had lost an eye in an explosion, he could identify the spectral patterns of all the elements. Marie knew that she had to collect enough of her new elements for Demarçay to put in his spectroscope so he could identify their new spectral lines.

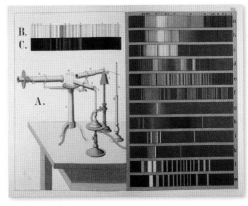

This diagram shows the basic structure of a spectroscope, along with the spectra emitted by several elements.

On July 18, 1898, Marie rushed into Demarçay's lab with a glass flask containing the day's radioactive yield—material associated with the bismuth batch. Demarçay put it into his spectroscope and saw a colored line he had never seen before, proof that she had found a new element. Marie named the element "polonium" after her beloved homeland.

Irène points to her mother's radium-scarred fingertips. Marie's fingertips were permanently damaged from handling radium.

Extracting enough polonium to measure its atomic weight, however, turned out to be too difficult. So Marie turned her attention to the other new element, which was associated with barium. Its radioactivity was so strong—900 times greater than uranium—that she named it "radium." The actual compound that Marie was trying to isolate was called radium chloride. At this point, it was dissolved in water with barium chloride. Since radium and barium were so similar chemically, finding a way to separate the two was a challenge. If a liquid containing both barium and radium chlorides (known as a solution) was allowed to evaporate, crystals formed. The first crystals that formed contained a higher proportion of radium chloride than the original solution, but they were not yet pure. The liquid remaining around the crystals was poured off. Then the crystals were redissolved in water, and the solution was allowed to crystallize again. Each time, the crystals contained more radium than before. This process was continued over and over again until pure radium chloride was obtained. The process was extremely tedious. That winter night in 1901, when Marie and Pierre visited their lab, the tables were covered with tiny evaporating dishes at different stages of this process of purification. It had been four years since they first started. Marie's fingers were permanently cracked and sore from her labors. Both she and Pierre complained of fatigue, aches, and pains. But they were close to the finish line. Marie just needed enough radium chloride to determine the atomic weight of radium.

Marie's lab was not the only place where interesting breakthroughs were being made. In the spring of 1897, just before Marie started her research project, an English scientist named J.J. Thomson was experimenting with a cathode-ray tube. Thomson was interested in the nature of the ray itself. When a cathode ray landed on the end of the tube opposite the cathode, the glass glowed with

J.J. Thomson (left) receives a medal from the British prime minister, honoring his discovery of the electron.

a green phosphorescence. A cross placed in the path of the cathode ray blocked it, so that a shadow of the cross was formed at the end of the tube. To Thomson, this was evidence that the cathode ray traveled in a straight line. Next, Thomson put a magnet around the ray. Surprisingly, the ray bent toward the positive pole of the magnet. This led Thomson to conclude that the ray was made up of a "wind" of tiny, negatively charged bodies of

The shadow of the cross in this cathode ray tube can be seen on the glass. This proved to Thomson that electrons travel in a straight line.

matter, which he called "corpuscles." Thomson was able to measure the mass of these corpuscles and found that they were more than a thousand times lighter than the hydrogen atom, the smallest and lightest of all atoms. Up to this point, scientists had thought that the atom was the smallest possible particle of matter, a hard little ball. (In fact, the word *atom* comes from a Greek word meaning "indivisible.") But here was something that looked like a piece of the atom. Thomson's corpuscles turned out to be quite common. They could be observed when certain metals were heated to high temperatures and when salts were put into flames. Today, we call Thomson's corpuscles "electrons" and we know that they are found in every atom on the periodic table.

Another interesting experiment had been done in Thomson's lab by Ernest Rutherford, a young scientist from New Zealand. Rutherford had put a magnet around a radioactive ray emitted by uranium. He found that the magnet split the ray into two parts. One part was not deflected by the magnet (it turned out that the magnet wasn't strong enough) and would penetrate thin metal foil. He called this part an "alpha ray." The other part of the ray was easily bent by the positive pole of the magnet and could penetrate metal 100 times thicker than was possible for alpha rays. He called this a "beta ray." It was eventually discovered that beta rays were made up of streams of electrons, just like cathode rays. Later, a third ray was discovered that could not be bent by a magnet. This was called a "gamma ray" and was extremely penetrating, very similar to an X-ray.

Ernest Rutherford is credited with the idea that most of the mass of an atom is in its postively charged nucleus.

These three rays produced by radioactive material became the tools scientists used to understand the structure of the atom, which in turn gave us a deep understanding of chemistry, light, electricity, magnetism, and the relationship between energy and matter.

chapter **8**

Rewards and Outcomes

Money was always a problem for the Curie household during the years Marie was working in the shed. Pierre scraped together an income from teaching part-time and tutoring. In the summer of 1900, Pierre was offered a professorship at the University of Geneva that included a well-equipped physics lab and a job for Marie. But he turned it down because Marie was so far along in her research and a move would delay her progress. A major discovery in science is always a competition, and Marie had a substantial lead in the race to isolate radium. Husband and wife agreed to stay in France. Two recent scientific meetings in Paris had put the Curies' work front and center in the international scientific community. This was no time to take a break.

Soon, Henri Poincaré, a brilliant French mathematician, came to

Pierre Curie performed many demonstrations of scientific principles for his students during his lectures as a professor at the Sorbonne.

the rescue. He helped Pierre obtain a teaching position at an annex of the Sorbonne's Faculty of Science, known as PCN. He also got Marie a teaching job at a government boarding school for teenage girls in the nearby Paris suburb of Sèvres. Marie's appointment caused a stir: Even though the school's purpose was to prepare bright young women to be teachers, she was the first woman to teach there. And she didn't even have her doctorate yet!

Marie sits with her students at Sèvres. She was the first teacher to include lab work as part of her instruction.

Both Marie and Pierre were inspiring teachers, and their students became very devoted to them. Although classes met only two or three times a week, preparation for these classes cut into the Curies' already-overscheduled lives. But at least they now had a financial cushion to relieve the relentless economic pressure of running a household and a lab. Even before obtaining their new jobs, the Curies had hired an assistant: a young chemist named André Debierne. In 1899, Debierne discovered yet another radioactive element, actinium, in the pitchblende residue. He would remain a lifelong associate of Marie's.

Meanwhile, Marie continued her research on the properties of radium. She gave Demarçay a sample so that

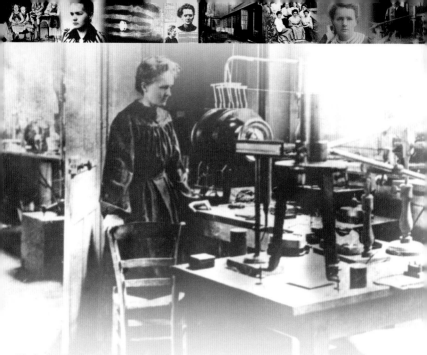

Marie continued studying radium while teaching and caring for her family. Like today's women, she had to juggle her responsibilities.

he could analyze its spectrum. She measured its atomic weight by comparing it to a known amount of silver chloride. On March 28, 1902, she made this historic record in her notebook: "Ra=225.93 the weight of an atom of radium." She found that all radium salts were luminous in the dark. She analyzed the radiation that came from radium and found that it gave off alpha, beta, and gamma rays. Its strength proved to be two million times stronger than uranium. She confirmed Rutherford's theory that alpha rays were heavy, positively charged particles, beta rays were like cathode rays, and gamma rays were like X-rays. She found that these rays could travel in air and in a vacuum and were very penetrating. Only a thick-walled lead container stopped all of them. Radioactivity made certain fluorescent chemicals glow in the dark. Radium made genuine diamonds luminous, and could therefore be used to detect fake ones. It spontaneously gave off heat. The glass containers that held the salts changed color to mauve and violet. Marie and Pierre found that many chemicals that were not originally radioactive became radioactive after being exposed to radium. They called this phenomenon induced radioactivity. But the part of Marie's research that caught the imagination of the world was the effect of radioactivity on human flesh.

Henri Becquerel had discovered that carrying around vials of radium salts in his pocket caused redness to appear on his skin, which could blister and act like a burn. Intrigued, Pierre conducted an experiment in which he put a weak radioactive salt on his arm for 10 hours. It caused an ulcerated burn that took four months to heal. If radium could destroy healthy tissue, could it also kill unhealthy tissue such as cancer? All kinds of possibilities opened up.

A steady stream of more than 30 papers published by the Curies between 1900 and 1903 let the world know of their findings. And the world took notice. The possible applications of radium, from cancer treatments to glow-in-the-

A radiation burn starts with redness to the skin. In extreme cases, a sore develops that takes months to heal.

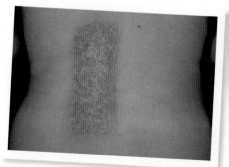

dark watch dials, caught the imagination of the public. Marie included the research from all her papers in her doctoral dissertation, which she defended in June 1903.

For a doctoral candidate, the defense of the dissertation is the last hurdle before receiving the degree. Marie's defense involved answering questions about her research posed by a jury of three professors, dressed in formal evening clothes. It was a momentous event. Bronya came from Poland and promptly marched Marie to a dress shop to purchase something new for the occasion. (Naturally, it was black and serviceable for the lab.) The oral examination took place in a small hall at the Sorbonne. It was a history-making event: Marie was the first female scientist to defend her thesis at the Sorbonne. The hall was packed with friends and family; even Marie's students from Sèvres attended. In clear, dispassionate language, Marie unhesitatingly answered every question posed by her professors. Occasionally she used a blackboard and chalk to write an equation or diagram a piece of apparatus. It was obvious she knew her subject better than anyone else in the room. In the end, her esteemed professor Mr. Lippmann

Professor Gabriel Lippmann was Marie's thesis advisor. He won a Nobel Prize in 1908 for his contributions to color photography.

formally prounounced, "The University of Paris accords you the title of doctor of physical science, with the mention *'très honorable'* [very high honors]." After the applause, Mr. Lippmann added with the warmth of an old friend, "And in the name of the jury, madame, I wish to express to you all our congratulations."

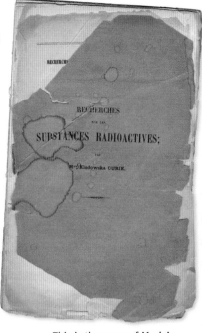

This is the cover of Marie's doctoral dissertation, titled "Research of Radioactive Substances."

That same day, by coincidence, Ernest Rutherford had arrived from England and dropped by the Curies' lab. He was informed that Marie was defending her dissertation at that very moment. He was too late to watch the event but he was invited to the small dinner party given in her honor that night by fellow physicist and colleague Paul Langevin. Marie's personality was very quiet and reserved, which some people interpreted as haughty or arrogant. Rutherford later said, "Madame Curie is a hard person to handle. She has at once the advantage and the inconvenience of being a woman." That statement may

> *"Madame Curie is a hard person to handle."*
>
> —Ernest Rutherford

have said more about him than it did about her.

When summer came, the Curies took a well-deserved vacation in the south of France. Marie, who had been expecting their second child, unfortunately had a miscarriage, which sent her into a depression.

The Curies also used this period of rest to make a decision about the future of radium. They could patent their method of purifying it, which would assure them a financial fortune. The money could be used to further their research and build a top-notch laboratory. On the other hand, they could publish their methods for the world to use as it wished. Marie didn't hesitate. "Physicists always publish their researches completely," she said to Pierre. "If our discovery has a commercial future, that is an accident by which we must not profit. And radium is going to be of use in treating disease. . . . It seems to me impossible to take advantage of that."

One scientist who did make a fortune from his invention was the Swedish industrialist Alfred Nobel, the inventor of dynamite. When he died, he left a trust worth nine million dollars, which would be used to award prizes each year to the people whose work was of the greatest benefit to mankind. The Nobel Prize was not only an honor but was accompanied by a substantial amount of cash. That summer, Pierre received a letter from the Swedish Academy of Sciences that he had been nominated for the award. There was no mention of Marie in the letter. So Pierre wrote back: "If it is true that one is seriously thinking about me, I very much wish to be considered together with Madame Curie with respect to our research on radioactive bodies."

The report that finally went to the

The Curies' Nobel Prize certificate recognized their research "on the radiation phenomena discovered by Professor Henri Becquerel."

The Nobel Prize made the Curies a popular subject for French media. Here they adorn the cover of a Parisian literary magazine.

Nobel committee on physics gave full credit to Marie for all her hard work. Since the award was given for their work on radioactivity itself, it was to be shared with Henri Becquerel. (Marie's work isolating radium was in the field of chemistry, not covered by this award.)

The Curies learned that they had won the Nobel Prize in mid-November. They were invited to Stockholm to receive the medal and give a lecture. But Pierre wrote back and said that their teaching obligations and Marie's poor health prevented them from coming until the following June. (Marie had not yet recovered from her depression.) This was only the third year that the Nobel Prizes had been in existence, and they hadn't acquired the enormous prestige they have today.

The money the Curies received put an end to their financial problems. Marie's one extravagance was to build a modern bathroom in her home. They could now afford an evening out at the theater or a concert. Most of the money was invested. The biggest change in their lives was the fame that had accompanied the prize. The press found the story irresistible: Marie was a poor Polish girl who married a reclusive French scientist, and together they worked to give the world an amazing new element. Requests for speaking engagements poured in, and reporters stalked them for interviews, as did well-meaning strangers. Marie wrote her brother Joseph: "Always a hubbub. People are keeping us from work as much as they can. Now I have decided to be brave and I receive no visitors—but they disturb me just the same. Our life has been altogether spoiled by honors and fame."

For years the Curies had been focused on work. Nothing interfered—not poverty, teaching obligations, their child, or the immense sorrow of family deaths (Marie's father had died in 1902). Only sudden fame finally disrupted their productive routines. The situation was not to their liking.

In the summers, the Curies often returned to the countryside, where they enjoyed a break from the pressures of the city.

chapter 9

Devastation

Pierre Curie had, according to his wife, "unshakable faith in science and in its power to further the general good of humanity." She also stated that, "he had dedicated his life to his dream of science: he felt the need of a companion who could live his dream with him. He told me many times that the reason he had not married until he was thirty-six was because he did not believe in the possibility of a marriage which would meet this, his absolute necessity." Pierre's thinking was so intense and so focused that he often failed to notice what was happening around him. He needed "to concentrate his thought with great intensity upon a certain definite object, in order to obtain a precise result." Nor could he interrupt or "modify the course of his reflections to suit exterior circumstances."

In accepting his Nobel Prize, Pierre said, "I am among those who think with Nobel that humanity will derive more good than bad from new discoveries."

This tended to make him appear absent minded and somehow remote to others. Once, after a dinner that Pierre had devoured with gusto, the cook asked if he had enjoyed the beefsteak he had just eaten. His answer was a bit confusing to her. "Did I eat beefsteak?" the scientist wondered aloud. "It's quite possible."

Pierre seemed to have no ego as a scientist. He didn't need credit for his own discoveries. Unlike Marie, he was not in a competitive race with others. What did it matter

When Pierre was away from his lab, he got restless. He was happiest when he was doing experiments.

who discovered some truth as long as it was proven by the highest standards of science? He was not capable of doing the backslapping and socializing that was necessary to ensure an appointment to a professorship. That's why he'd only taught in lesser institutions so far, not the great Sorbonne. (The PCN was associated with the Sorbonne, but his position there was less prestigious than one at the main part of the university.) He believed strongly that his work spoke for itself and he had no problem deferring to his wife in those areas where he felt that she outshone him.

After winning the Nobel Prize, however, things started to change. Pierre was nominated for the Academy of Sciences,

the most prestigious of French scientific institutions. He had been rejected for membership earlier, before he won the prize, and he had hated the round of visits he had been required to make before the unsuccessful vote. In 1905, he was finally admitted, although he never did understand the point of it. He wrote to a colleague: "I have not yet discovered what is the use of the Academy." Marie, unfortunately, was not eligible for membership because it was for men only.

Pierre's single demand, when it came to his teaching jobs, was a laboratory where he could continue his research. In the winter of 1904 he was offered a full professorship at the Sorbonne. Here at last was the teaching position he most desired. Yet he turned it down when he found out that there was no laboratory included in the offer. After some negotiation, the university agreed to build two rooms for Pierre at an inconvenient location, not near the lecture hall. The only concession that really pleased him was that the university would hire three coworkers for him: a laboratory assistant, an aide, and the head of his lab—and this last role was to be filled by his wife. For the first time, Marie would have a paid position in her husband's laboratory. In addition, she would be the first woman to hold such a position at the Sorbonne. So the Curies gave up their old shed to become official partners in science. Although their ultimate dream was a modern, fully equipped and staffed laboratory, these two new rooms were a step in the right direction. On the home front, the Curies' everyday routine had expanded to include their second daughter, Eve, born on December 6, 1904. Life was hectic but fulfilling.

Marie, Irène, and Pierre pose in their backyard garden. Gardening was an important form of relaxation for Marie.

The morning of April 19, 1906, started out like many others. Marie

was getting breakfast for Irène and dressing Eve. As he rushed out the door, Pierre asked Marie if she was going to the laboratory that day, and she replied that she would probably not have time. Pierre's schedule included lunch with some professors and an afternoon appointment with his publisher to correct a manuscript. That evening, their old friend, Polish physicist Joseph Kovalski, was coming to dinner. Pierre fondly remembered how Joseph had been responsible for introducing him to Marie. It rained hard that day, and the Paris streets were crowded with black umbrellas.

That afternoon, Pierre was rushing from lunch to his publisher. A block from his destination, as he stepped out from behind a carriage to cross the street, he moved blindly into the path of a heavy cart drawn by two large horses. There was no way for the driver to stop. Pierre was knocked to the ground and killed instantly as the left wheel of the cart struck his head.

Although the automobile was gaining popularity, draft horses were still used to transport heavy loads through Paris streets in 1906.

He was identified by the police from the calling cards in his pocket. They immediately informed Dean Paul Appell of the Sorbonne of the tragedy. The dean and Professor Jean Perrin, the Curies' best friend and neighbor, went to the Curie home to break the news of the catastrophe.

The Perrins were the Curies' closest friends, as can be seen in this group photo from 1902.

When they arrived, only Pierre's father was home with the baby. Marie had gone off for the day with Irène. Dr. Curie guessed what had happened from the men's faces the instant he opened the door. "My son is dead," he said. "What was he dreaming of this time?"

Marie returned at 6:00 PM. The news had an unreal feel to it. "Pierre is dead? Dead? Absolutely dead?" she asked. Dry-eyed and gray-faced, she asked Jean Perrin's wife, Henrietta, to take Irène for a few days. (Eve was too young to know what was happening.) She sent Bronya a brief telegram: "Pierre dead result accident." And she waited for Pierre's body to be brought home. When it arrived, she kissed it until friends made her leave the room so they could bathe and dress it. The next day, the newspapers were full of stories on this immense loss to science and to the world. Hundreds

> *"This laboratory provides me with the illusion that I am holding on to a piece of your life . . ."*
>
> —Marie Curie

of letters poured in to the young widow, who walked through her days like a zombie.

Sitting alone with his coffin, Marie felt his presence: "I put my head against [the coffin] . . . and I spoke to you. I told you that I loved you and that I had always loved you with all my heart . . . And it seemed to me that from this cold contact of my forehead with the casket something came to me, something like a calm and an intuition that I would yet find the courage to live. Was this an illusion or was this an accumulation of energy coming from you and condensing in the closed casket which came to me?" When she first went to the lab 11 days after the tragedy, she began a journal: "Dear Pierre," she wrote, "who I will never more see here, I want to speak to you in the silence of this laboratory, where I never thought I would have to live without you."

Slowly, Marie found her way back into life. She had her two young children to take care of. Dr. Curie remained in her home and they could comfort each other. She went to the laboratory. She continued to write in her journal as if she were speaking directly to her husband: "I am better there than anywhere else. . . . Still this laboratory provides me with the illusion that I am holding on to a piece of your life and the evidence of your passage. I found again a little picture of you next to the scales . . . of such a nice smiling expression that I can't see it without sobs rising in my chest." The French government offered Marie a pension as the widow of such an illustrious scientist. She turned it down flat: "I don't want a pension. I am young enough to earn my living and that of my children."

The month after Pierre's death, the science faculty at the Sorbonne met to determine what to do about replacing him. Sweeping away traditions and customs, they decided to ask Marie to take the position, which would make her the first woman ever to be a professor at the Sorbonne. Friends urged her to accept, knowing that work was the best therapy for her grief. Although she did take the job, she still had mixed feelings. She wrote in her journal: "I don't know if it is good or bad. . . . Sometimes it seems to me that that's the way it will be easiest for me to live, other times it seems to me that I am crazy to undertake that. How many

Despite her grief, Marie Curie resolved to continue working on alone after her husband's tragic death at age 46.

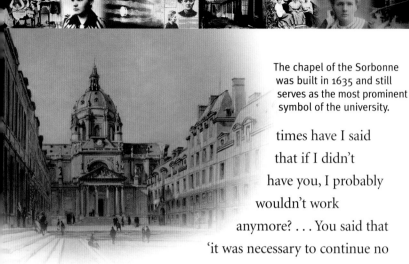

times have I said that if I didn't have you, I probably wouldn't work anymore? . . . You said that 'it was necessary to continue no matter what.'" She spent the summer in Paris, working in the lab and preparing her lectures for the upcoming course that fall. Irène was sent to Poland to visit her aunts, and Dr. Curie took Eve to the south of France.

Marie's first lecture at the Sorbonne was scheduled for 1:30 PM on November 5, 1906. The lecture hall held only 120 people and it was packed, standing room only, the moment it opened at noon. Seats had been reserved for Marie's advanced class from Sèvres. The newspaper reported: "The front rows looked like the orchestra seats of a theater. Formal dresses, a profusion of large hats; fortunately the hall is built in tiers!" The atmosphere was electric. What would the grieving widow say to honor her husband? Since this was the first lecture of the term, the dean would traditionally introduce the professor and speak about her predecessor. At 1:20, Dean Appell made the announcement that, at the request of Madame Curie, there would be no official introduction and no eulogy for Pierre. Marie entered the hall promptly at 1:30 and waited through a standing ovation with lowered eyes. Then, in a soft, matter-of-fact voice, which still had a faint Polish accent, she said: "When one considers the progress that has been made in physics in the past ten years, one is surprised at the advance that has taken place in ideas concerning electricity and matter." These words were a direct quote from the final sentences of Pierre Curie's last lecture. She simply continued on with his lesson, discussing new theories on ions, atomic disintegration, and radioactive substances straight to the end. Her forthright manner and dispassionate delivery strangely emphasized the courage it took to give the lecture. When she was finished, she quietly picked up her notes and exited the room. Who would have thought that a lecture on physics could produce so many tears?

Marie Curie lectures to a packed house. It soon became obvious that she was more than capable of filling her husband's shoes.

10
Life Goes On

Four months after Pierre's death, a letter from Lord Kelvin appeared in the London *Times*. Kelvin was an astute and respected scientist, and had been an early admirer of Pierre Curie's work with piezoelectricity. This made the content of his letter even more surprising: He was publicly challenging the Curies' discovery of radium. He claimed that radium was probably a molecular compound of lead and helium, and that the Curies had mistakenly taken it for a new element. Kelvin further implied that they did not deserve the Nobel Prize. Although Ernest Rutherford rushed to defend the Curies, Marie saw that her only defense would be to produce pure, metallic radium—an extremely difficult task. She returned to her lab with a vengeance. Her anger over Lord Kelvin's criticism fueled her efforts and helped with her grief. It took four years, but she managed to produce

Lord Kelvin is best known for developing a scale of temperature based on absolute zero, the point at which all molecular motion ceases.

a few grains of silvery radium metal. Unfortunately, Lord Kelvin died before he knew his error.

Shortly after Marie assumed Pierre's teaching duties at the Sorbonne, she had met American steel millionaire Andrew Carnegie. He was so impressed with her that he sent Dean Appell $50,000 to establish a foundation that would fund scholarships and a laboratory. Carnegie stipulated that it be

Marie sits pensively in her laboratory, surrounded by pieces of scientific equipment.

named the Curies Foundation. "Making it plural," he explained, "will include Madame, which I am most anxious to do." This sum, which was substantial at that time, enabled Marie to start building the laboratory that she and Pierre had dreamed of.

Marie's other main concern was the education of her daughters. Feeling that the city air was unhealthy, she moved the family to Sceaux, Pierre's hometown, in the summer of 1906, adding an hour's commute to her day. Her father-in-law continued to live with the family to help with the girls, and Marie also hired a series of Polish governesses so that her children could learn her native language. Although she had excelled as a student under difficult circumstances, Marie was of the firm opinion that learning should be a joyous experience. She didn't think much of French schools:

In 1906, Marie moved her family to this house in Sceaux, Pierre's hometown. She felt the country was a better place for children.

"In most schools, as they exist today, the time spent in various reading and writing exercises is too great, and the study required to be done at home too much. . . . Next to outdoor walks, I attach a great importance to gymnastics and sports." She prevailed on her closest friends, the Perrins and Paul Langevin, who had children about the same age as Irène, to help her create an informal school. There would be only one lesson every day, but it would be taught by a master from the Sorbonne or else by one of the parents themselves. The children would learn chemistry, mathematics, physics, art, French literature, and history. They would visit museums and go to concerts. This experiment in learning lasted two years, and was remembered fondly by all its participants. After that, the girls were enrolled in private schools. Irène was very much her father's daughter and was destined to become a distinguished scientist in her own right. Eve was much more social than her older sister and showed exceptional talent as a pianist.

Marie was not a physically affectionate mother, perhaps because her own mother had been too ill to hug and kiss her. There was little or no mention of Pierre in the home.

Marie could not speak of her own feelings and presented a controlled, intellectual face to the world and to her children. Her behavior masked a passionate and loving woman who had been wounded by losses. The early loss of her mother and sister, the death of her father, and the tragic loss of her husband had taught her how to go through the motions of living while grieving privately. She poured out her feelings in her journal and in letters to her siblings. Unfortunately, the family was to suffer yet another loss when Dr. Curie died in 1910, at the age of 82. This death was particularly hard on Irène, who had been very close to her grandfather. In spite of Marie's remoteness, her daughters never doubted their mother's love for them and later credited her for preparing them well for life.

This picture was taken two years after Pierre's death. Jacques Curie commented on how sad Marie looked.

Marie was only 39 years old when she was widowed, still a young woman. One evening, in April 1910, she appeared at a friend's dinner party in a new white dress with a rose at her waist. Clearly, she was feeling better about life. Always careful to keep her private life

Marie's relationship with the married Paul Langevin caused a scandal in the French press in 1911.

private, only her closest friends could guess what was behind the transformation. Marie had a new love interest: fellow physicist and mathematician Paul Langevin.

Unfortunately, for Marie, Paul was married with four children. The scientists who taught at the Sorbonne were a closeknit group who worked together and socialized together. Paul's marital troubles were no secret to the group. His wife wanted him to get a job that paid better than teaching. He preferred the intense stimulation of physics. A new idea about the structure of the atom was on the horizon. Chemistry and physics were coming together. It was the most exciting time to be a physical scientist. A strong professional friendship with Marie Curie was blossoming into romance.

At that place and time, a marriage was not something that was split up easily. Divorce was almost unheard of. Although Paul's marriage was very unhappy and he lived separately from his family for a time, his wife was very much opposed to giving him a divorce. He confided to Marie about his marital situation, which was becoming disruptive to his work. Marie may have dreamed of a partnership with a fellow scientist, like she had experienced with Pierre. She may even have discussed this possibility with Paul. But it was not going to happen. Mrs. Langevin caught wind of the relationship, accosted Marie on the street, and threatened to kill her if she didn't leave France. This was so upsetting to Marie that she and Paul decided not to see each other socially for a while.

Nevertheless, their professional relationship continued. In the fall of 1911, the two scientists attended an international physics conference in Brussels. The fact that 20 others also attended the conference did not comfort Paul's angry wife. In fact, the conference apparently pushed Mrs. Langevin over the edge, and she went to the newspapers with the scandal. The idea of a love triangle involving an acclaimed female scientist was

Marie sits in the front row at the Solvay Conference. Paul Langevin is on the far right, next to Albert Einstein.

CONSEIL DE PHYSIQUE SOLVAY
BRUXELLES 1911
HOTEL METROPOLE

GOLDSCHMIDT PLANCK RUBENS LINDEMANN HASENOHRL
NERNST BRILLOUIN SOMMERFELD DE BROGLIE HOSTELET
SOLVAY KNUDSEN HERZEN JEANS RUTHERFORD
LORENTZ WARBURG WIEN EINSTEIN LANGEVIN
PERRIN MME CURIE POINCARE KAMERLINGH ONNES

irresistible to the press. There were headlines in all the papers making mostly false accusations about Marie, including claims that she had run off with Paul. Marie wrote an indignant denial of wrongdoing to one newspaper. Nevertheless, the publicity had done its damage. There was talk of removing her from her teaching post at the Sorbonne. Marie's close friends rallied around her. Since many of them were also on the faculty, their defense was effective. She did not lose her job.

At the height of the negative publicity, Marie was suddenly in the news for quite a different reason. She had won the Nobel Prize for chemistry—this time all by herself. The award was for her accurate determination of the atomic weight of radium and for isolating it in metallic form. A member of the Nobel Committee, however, wrote and asked her not to come to Sweden to receive the award because of the scandal. It was not an official proclamation, but it was still insulting. She answered: "The Prize has been awarded for discovery of Radium and Polonium. I believe that

Marie and Paul Langevin taught together at the school at Sèvres. Here they pose for a photograph with some students.

there is no connection between my scientific work and the facts of private life . . . I cannot accept the idea in principle that the appreciation of the value of scientific work should be influenced by libel and slander concerning private life."

Despite her determination, these problems took their toll on Marie's health. She was losing weight, and friends worried that she might not be strong enough to make the two-day trip to Stockholm for the

Published during the Langevin scandal, this newspaper paints Marie in an unflattering light, despite her many achievements.

award ceremony. Gathering her strength, she made the journey, taking Bronya and Irène with her. With her head held high, in a simple black lace dress, she delivered her lecture to the Nobel Academy, the first woman ever to do so. She was generous in her acknowledgments of the work done by other scientists, which had contributed to her findings. But she gave herself full credit for the painstaking and delicate measurements that had ended up establishing a new field of science, one that probed the secrets of the atom itself. Upon returning to Paris, Marie became so ill with kidney problems that Bronya had her admitted to a private clinic, where she recuperated, hidden from the press, under the name Madame Marya Sklodowska.

11

War and the Little Curies

It took Marie more than a year to recover from her illness. By this point, she may have suspected that exposure to radium had caused some of her health problems, but that suspicion would not keep her from her research. While convalescing over the summer of 1912, she was visited by Albert Einstein and his family. The two scientists had a lot to discuss. What was the source of this immense energy that came from radioactive elements? All radioactive elements had high atomic weights. What did this have to do with radioactivity? Marie and Einstein talked about this endlessly.

Part of Marie's convalescence had been spent in England at the home of Hertha Ayrton. Like Marie, Hertha was both a scientist and the widow of a scientist. Obviously, they had a lot in common. Hertha was also very active politically, fighting for the right of women to vote.

Marie and Albert Einstein enjoyed their long walks. At the time, Einstein was not the scientific celebrity that he would become later in life.

Women's Suffrage

In both Britain and the United States, women were fighting for the right to vote, also known as suffrage. British activist Emmiline Pankhurst incited riots and went on hunger strikes to keep the issue in front of the public. Great Britain gave women over 30 the right to vote in 1918, and all women over 18 won the right in 1928. The 19th Amendment gave women in the United States the right to vote in 1920.

(Marie was sympathetic to the cause, but she was too busy with her research to be an activist.) Hertha always became angry when members of the scientific community assumed that her husband and Marie's had been the ones who did the significant work while the wives were only helpers. When a British newspaper said that radium had been discovered by Pierre Curie, Hertha wrote the newspaper to stick up for her friend: "Errors are notoriously hard to kill," she wrote, "but an error that ascribes to a man what was actually the work of a woman, has more lives than a cat."

Marie finally got back to work in the fall of 1912. By the following spring, ground had been broken for the new French Radium Institute on a street named for Pierre and Marie Curie. It was to be a fully operational

Marie visited her siblings in Warsaw in 1912. Marie is on the left next to Bronya. Hela sits next to Joseph.

research center, and Marie would serve as the director of the lab. The summer would be spent with the girls and many of her friends in L'Arcouest, a peaceful fishing village on the northwest coast of France, in the province of Brittany. Marie was productive and healthy again.

One year later, things were much the same. Marie had sent the girls on ahead of her to L'Arcouest while she put the finishing touches on her new lab. The flowers in the garden surrounding the Radium Institute were blooming. Then, on July 28, 1914, the heir to the Austrian throne and his wife were assassinated in Sarajevo, Bosnia. This lit a fire in the Balkan States that spread throughout Europe. The Serbian army mobilized, as did those of Germany, Austria, and Russia.

Gavrilo Princip (second from left) is arrested following the assassination of Archduke Ferdinand and his wife.

On August 4, World War I began. It would kill 20 million people. Poland was invaded. Britain declared war on Germany. Paris was no longer safe. Marie left the children in Brittany. The French government moved its offices to Bordeaux, in the south of France. Shortly afterward, Marie made a trip to Bordeaux herself.

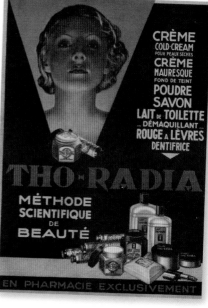

This ad promotes a full line of radium-based beauty products: face cream, powder, toothpaste, lipstick, and more.

Radium had become extremely expensive. First, preparing it from ore was a long and arduous task. Second, people had found commercial uses for it. Combined with a fluorescent mineral, it created a luminous paint that glowed in the dark. Since it could destroy abnormal growths on the skin, doctors believed it could cure cancer (they didn't know then that it could also cause it) as well as maintain good general health. Radium drinking solution and radium face powder were popular items. Spinthariscopes, devices that displayed tiny flashes of light caused by alpha particles, became a fashionable curiosity and were given as gifts. The demand for radium on the open market was at an all-time high.

Russian soldiers lie dead after a battle in Poland in 1915. Historians estimate that nearly 20 million people died in the war.

Marie had shared some of her radium with other scientists to further the study of radioactivity. Some of it had been used to establish the standard unit of measurement for radioactivity. The precious supply of radium that she had left in her lab was considered a national treasure, and Marie was responsible for its safekeeping. With the Germans breathing down the necks of Parisians, Marie packed up her gram of radium (about half a teaspoon) in a 45-pound (20 kg) lead container and boarded a train for Bordeaux, where she would leave her priceless stash in a bank vault until the war was over. On the way down, the train was full of civilians traveling away from Paris to safety. On her return

trip the next day, the train was
filled with soldiers—young men
preparing to fight on the bloodiest
battlefields the world had ever

seen. She preferred the company on her return home.

Poland was now a battleground between Germany
and Russia. Communications between Marie and her
family were cut off. Since there was nothing she could do
for her beloved homeland, Marie directed her energies
toward helping her adopted country. As a physicist,
she knew how to produce X-rays and she knew how X-
rays could save lives. Namely, they could show doctors
where bullets and shrapnel had buried themselves in
human flesh. Doctors could then use this information to
operate more swiftly and precisely. Marie began setting
up radiology units in hospitals using equipment that
was sitting around in labs and in the offices of doctors
who had gone off to war. However, it soon became clear

to her that X-ray
units had to be more
mobile, so that they
could be brought to
the field hospitals
just behind the front

X-rays, like this one showing
a gunshot wound to the arm,
saved many lives during
World War I.

lines where the battles were being fought. In war, the sooner the wounded got medical attention, the better.

First, Marie got the Red Cross to donate a car and some money for X-ray equipment, which she figured would weigh about 500 pounds (227 kg). Since electricity was needed to

produce X-rays, she found a generator that ran off the car engine. All the equipment was mounted in the little car. On November 1, 1914, when the first radiology car set off, it

was staffed with a trained doctor, a technician, and a driver. Marie also came along, as did Irène, now 17 and chomping at the bit to help her mother. It was not a moment too soon—310,000 Frenchmen had already died and 300,000 more had been wounded.

Marie Curie and her daughter Irène initially worked as a team bringing X-ray machines to hospitals for soldiers wounded in battle.

Marie Curie drove a "little Curie" fitted out with radiological equipment to hospitals near the front.

When the team arrived at their destination, the technician and the doctor unloaded the table and set the equipment up while the driver hooked up a long cable to the generator. Within half an hour, they were ready to start. Marie wrote: "[Examining patients] lasts as long as is necessary, time is forgotten, all that matters is getting the job done with care. Sometimes, a difficult case slows things down, other times, the work proceeds rapidly. Finally the task is finished. The team packs the equipment in the cases and returns to its base, to begin again the same day or else the next."

In total, Marie equipped and trained the staff for 20 cars, known as "the little Curies." In addition, she equipped and staffed 200 permanent radiology posts in hospitals.

She trained women to be radiologists as well as men. Before long, Irène was working independently from her mother. She later wrote: "My mother had just as much confidence in me as she had in herself." In the last two years of the war, more than a million soldiers were x-rayed and many were saved because Marie Curie had found a way to change French battlefield medicine.

chapter 12

A Trip to America

After the war was over, Marie was anxious to get back to her lab and resume her research. She decided that the mission of the Radium Institute should be to fill in as many blanks as possible in the study of radioactivity. Unfortunately, the institute was in bad shape. Much of the equipment had disappeared during the war and many of the science students who would have been candidates to work in her lab had not returned to school. Marie received an official letter from the French minister of finance offering assistance, but it was clear that there were other demands on the government that would take priority. The problem of funding her research was more critical than ever. How could she get some money? Marie was always turning down interviews with the press. Ever since the

Surrounded by scientific literature, Marie Curie occupied this office at the Radium Institute from 1914 until her death in 1934.

The Radium Institute was founded to study radioactivity. Although construction started in 1912, it wasn't fully operational until 1919.

Langevin scandal, she regarded reporters as her enemies. However, one morning in May 1920, she was introduced through a mutual friend to an American journalist named Missy Mattingly, who was editor-in-chief of a respected women's magazine. The two women hit it off right away, and Marie began to let down her guard as Missy interviewed her. When Missy asked Marie what she wanted most in the world, Marie unhesitatingly said, "A gram of radium." Marie might as well have asked for the moon. A gram of radium cost $100,000, a great deal of money in 1920. But Missy thought she might be able to raise the money from wealthy Americans. Marie had an appealing story: Here was the woman who discovered radium, considered the cure for cancer, who had nobly refused to profit from her discovery and was in desperate need of some radium to continue her work. Missy explained that she would have to use Marie's famous name to accomplish this goal and Marie would have to come to America to claim the gram of radium. Marie agreed. Einstein had once said, "Marie Curie is, of all celebrated beings, the only one whom fame has not corrupted." Marie may not have been corrupted by fame, but she was a realist and determined to continue

her work. There was no time to waste if she was to get back into the game of science.

By this point, the game was more exciting than ever. Over the last several years, scientists' understanding of radioactivity and the structure of the atom had grown by leaps and bounds. In 1902, Ernest Rutherford and his colleague Frederick Soddy had proposed a new theory of radioactivity: When an atom gave off an alpha particle, it changed into another element. In other words, the

Niels Bohr is considered the father of modern atomic theory, which explains the properties of the elements.

atom decayed. Uranium was the beginning of a long series of radioactive elements—each atom that emitted an alpha particle became another "daughter" element. The chain of decay was uranium, thorium, radium, radon, polonium, and finally lead. Lead was not radioactive and was therefore stable. This meant that any sample of radioactive material was a mixture of several elements at different stages along this chain of decay. The decay chain was complicated because there were a number of smaller steps in which beta and gamma rays were emitted but no alpha rays. Some of these intermediate atoms had the same chemical properties as uranium or radium, but had slightly different atomic

Half-life

Some radioactive elements seem to run down after a while. Rutherford measured how long it took for half of the atoms in a sample of radioactive element to give up their rays. He called this measurement "half-life." Uranium has a half-life of 4.5 billion years. Radium has a half-life of 1,600 years. Radon gas has a half-life of almost four days.

weights. Soddy called these variations "isotopes."

In 1909, Rutherford proposed that most of the weight of an atom was centered in a very small and very dense nucleus that had a positive electrical charge. J.J. Thompson had already discovered the extremely light, negatively charged electron. Since opposite charges attract each other, the nucleus should have attracted the electrons and its charge should have been canceled out. Yet this didn't happen. What was the force that kept the electrons from colliding with the nucleus? In 1913, Danish physicist Niels Bohr proposed a model of the atom based on the simplest atom, hydrogen. The hydrogen atom consisted of a positive nucleus with an atomic weight of one. Its single electron orbited the nucleus at high speed like a planet in a miniature solar system. The speed of the electron

The Bohr atom consists of a positive nucleus surrounded by orbiting electrons.

kept it from crashing into the nucleus, just as the speed of the earth keeps it from crashing into the sun. The Bohr model of the atom explained how atoms combined to form molecules, why elements were arranged so neatly on the periodic table, and how atoms turned into ions by losing or gaining electrons. In short, this brilliant understanding of the atom, now known as modern atomic theory, brought together

Marie and her daughters arrive in New York. Pictured here from left to right are Missy Mattingly, Irène, Marie, and Eve.

chemistry and physics and became the cornerstone of 20th-century science. Through her study of radioactivity, Marie had opened the door to a new field: nuclear physics, the study of the nucleus of the atom.

In this fast-paced scientific climate, it was no wonder that Marie wanted her radium. Luckily, Missy Mattingly was as good as her word. She started a national subscription to the Marie Curie Radium Fund. The publicity made Americans eager to meet the renowned French scientist. Once the funds had been raised, President Warren G. Harding would present Marie with the gram of radium at a White House reception.

One year after her first meeting with Missy, Marie and her daughters set sail for the United States. They were to tour the country, meet with scientists and philanthropists, and visit with dignitaries for a period of six weeks. Marie was overwhelmed by the reception. Her shy nature was not prepared for the enthusiastic crowds and overly zealous press. She sent her daughters to stand in for her at many events. One admirer squeezed her hand so hard that she had to wear a splint to the reception at the White House. There, President Harding presented her with the key to a lead-lined box weighing 110 pounds (50 kg) containing one gram of precious radium. In addition, Marie received another $22,000 in precious minerals, including thorium, almost $7,000 in various fees, and $52,000 that was left over from the fund. Marie had agreed that Missy could write her biography and for this she received another $50,000. This was more than enough to fund her institute. Marie returned home convinced more than ever that science was the only key to progress.

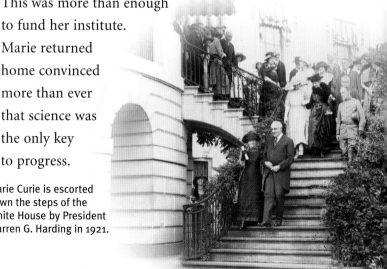

Marie Curie is escorted down the steps of the White House by President Warren G. Harding in 1921.

13

Marie Curie's Legacy

Marie Curie died on July 4, 1934, with her daughter Eve by her side. She was 66 years old. She had lived long enough to see her daughter Irène and Irène's husband, Frédéric Joliot-Curie, become distinguished scientists in her lab. They had been beaten to the finish line in two major discoveries, and Marie was rooting for them to be the first in making the next one. In January 1934, Irène and Frédéric were conducting an experiment that involved bombarding aluminum with alpha particles. Some aluminum atoms "captured" an alpha particle and turned into a radioactive isotope of phosphorus. They had created a new kind of radioactive element, one that didn't exist in nature! Immediately, they informed Marie, who came over right away. Frédéric later wrote: "I will never forget the expression of intense joy which

Marie Curie leans thoughtfully on the railing of the balcony outside her office at the Radium Institute in 1934, near the end of her life.

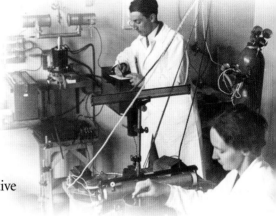

Here, Irène and Frédéric Joliot-Curie are shown at work in their lab at the Radium Institute.

overtook her when Irène and I showed her the first [artificially produced] radioactive element in a little glass tube. I can see her still taking this little tube of the radioelement, already quite weak, in her radium-damaged fingers. To verify what we were telling her, she brought the Geiger counter up close to it and she could hear the numerous clicks. This was without a doubt the last great satisfaction of her life."

On the personal side, Marie Curie had been a pioneer—a working mother in a man's world. She made certain that her children always had loving care, even if she wasn't always the one to provide it. And her children turned out just fine. Irène had married and had a son and a daughter, beloved grandchildren for Marie to dote on. Irène and Frédéric won the Nobel Prize in 1935 for their discovery of artificial radioactivity. Eve became a musician and writer; her biography of her mother was a best-seller. Later, she married a diplomat and became involved in many philanthropic activities.

GEIGER COUNTER

A Geiger counter is a device that measures radioactivity by making a clicking sound.

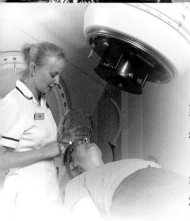

This patient is about to undergo radiotherapy, which uses ionizing radiation to destroy cancerous tumors in the body.

As a teacher, Marie trained hundreds of brilliant scientists in the procedures that she had invented. She called these scientists her "children."

Marie Curie was honored many times during her life. She received eight major prizes (including the two Nobel Prizes), sixteen medals and decorations, as well as more than a hundred honorary degrees and doctorates. In 1995, the bodies of Marie and Pierre Curie were moved from the quiet cemetery in Sceaux to the Panthéon in France, where the nation's most honored heroes are interred.

Throughout her life, Marie suffered from fatigue, backaches, kidney problems, and cataracts. She died of a type of leukemia. We now know that radioactivity caused many of her health problems. She may have suspected that radium was making her sick, but she never let that get in the way of her work. Some doctors think she was lucky to have given birth to two healthy children, considering her level of exposure to radioactivity. Today, anyone who works with radioactive materials takes precautions to prevent direct exposure. Radium itself is no longer used in medicine; many new isotopes have proven to be safer and more effective. Still, the dosage of radioactivity a patient receives is measured in "curies."

When Marie Curie set a goal for herself, she let nothing stop her from achieving it. Poverty didn't stop her from getting an education. Marriage only enhanced her personal growth; it didn't stop it. Children didn't stop her from pursuing a career, and her career didn't stop her from being a good mother. Lack of money didn't stop her from building up the Radium Institute into the world's premier laboratory for research into radioactivity. Illnesses, off and on throughout her life, didn't stop her. Grief and the loss of a beloved partner didn't stop her. Above all, being female at a time when women were second-class citizens who didn't even have the right to vote didn't stop her. She was in the news because of her achievements, and because she was a woman she became a target for the press. Although it cost her great pain, even notoriety didn't stop her. She had very high standards for her own ethical behavior—she was not tempted by fame or the possibility of fortune. Marie Curie was an extraordinarily honorable person, a truly worthy role model for generations to come.

This statue of Marie Curie was installed outside another Radium Institute she helped establish, in Warsaw, Poland.

MARJI
SKŁODOWSKIEJ · CURIE
STOLICA

Events in the Life of Marie Curie

1884–1890
Marie works as
a governess.

June 1903
Marie defends her
thesis at the Sorbonne.

July 26, 1895
Marie marries
Pierre Curie.

November 7, 1867
Marya (Marie)
Sklodowska is born
in Warsaw, Poland.

July–December 1898
Marie Curie discovers
two new elements, which she
names polonium and radium.

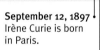

May 1878
Marie's mother dies.

September 12, 1897
Irène Curie is born
in Paris.

November 1903
Marie and Pierre
Curie share the
third Nobel Prize
in Physics with
Henri Becquerel
for the discovery
of radioactivity.

November 1891
Marie goes to
Paris to study at
the Sorbonne.

December 16, 1897
Marie and Pierre begin
work on uranium salts.

May 1906
Marie becomes the first female professor at the Sorbonne.

October 9, 1926
Irène marries Frédéric Joliot.

1915–1918
Marie and Irène develop and operate mobile X-ray units to treat soldiers in World War I.

April 19, 1906
Pierre Curie is killed in a traffic accident.

January 1934
Irène and Frédéric Joliot-Curie discover artificial radioactivity.

October 1911
Marie Curie attends the first Solvay Conference in Brussels, and wins the Nobel Prize for Chemistry.

May 1921
Marie visits the United States to raise money.

Spring 1912
Ground is broken on the French Radium Institute.

December 6, 1904
Eve Curie is born.

July 3, 1934
Marie Curie dies in the French Alps.

Bibliography

Books

Balchin, Jon. *Science: 100 Scientists Who Changed the World*. New York: Enchanted Lion Books, 2003.

Birch, Beverly. *Marie Curie: Courageous Pioneer in the Study of Radioactivity*. Woodbridge, Connecticut: Blackbirch Press, 2000.

Brian, Denis. *The Curies: A Biography of the Most Controversial Family in Science*. Hoboken, NJ: John Wiley & Sons, 2005.

Curie, Eve. *Madame Curie: A Biography*. New York: Doubleday, 1937.

Curie, Marie. *Pierre Curie*. New York: Dover, 1963.

Curie, Marie. *Radioactive Substances*. Mineola, NY: Dover, 2002.

Giroud, Françoise. *Marie Curie: A Life*. Translated by Lydia Davis. New York: Holmes & Meier, 1986.

Goldsmith, Barbara. *Obsessive Genius: The Inner World of Marie Curie*. New York: W. W. Norton, 2005.

Helibron, J. L. *Ernest Rutherford and the Explosion of Atoms*. New York: Oxford University Press, 2003.

Holton, Gerald and Duane H. D. Roller, *Foundations of Modern Physical Science*. Reading, MA: Addison-Wesley, 1958.

Lassieur, Allison. *Marie Curie: A Scientific Pioneer*. New York: Franklin Watts, 2003.

McClafferty, Carla Killough. *Something Out of Nothing: Marie Curie and Radium*. New York: Farrar Straus, & Giroux, 2006.

Pflaum, Rosalynd. *Grand Obsession: Madame Curie and Her World*. New York: Doubleday, 1989.

Quinn, Susan. *Marie Curie: A Life*. New York: Simon & Schuster, 1995.

Films

Marie Curie: More Than Meets the Eye. Devine Entertainment, 1997.
Madame Curie, MGM, 1943.

Works Cited

p.8: "You know, Bronya . . ." *Madame Curie: A Biography*, 176

p.8: "I wonder what It will be like . . ." *Madame Curie: A Biography*, 157

p.9: "Don't light the lamps . . ." *Madame Curie: A Biography*, 171

p.11: "Beg—pardon! Pardon! I didn't do it on purpose . . ." *Madame Curie: A Biography*, 9

p.13: "My father . . . even composed poetry himself . . ." *Pierre Curie*, 79

p.14: "This catastrophe was the first great sorrow . . ." *Pierre Curie*, 78

p.16: "Please call on one of these young people." *Madame Curie: A Biography*, 19

p.17: "His Majesty Alexander II . . ." *Madame Curie: A Biography*, 21

p.18: "All instruction was given in Russian . . ." *Pierre Curie*, 79

p.18: "I learned easily mathematics and physics . . ." *Pierre Curie*, 80

p.19: "We go out in a band to walk in the woods . . ." *Madame Curie: A Biography*, 40

p.21: "I have been to a kulig . . ." *Madame Curie: A Biography*, 43

p.21: "The summer passes . . ." Quinn, *Marie Curie: A Life*, 33

p.25: "I have seven hours of work a day: . . ." *Madame Curie: A Biography*, 64–67

p.26: "The Z. household is relatively cultivated . . ." *Madame Curie: A Biography*, 67

p 26: "These solitary studies were encompassed . . ." *Madame Curie: A Biography*, 72

p.28: "For now that I have lost the hope of ever becoming anybody . . ." *Madame Curie: A Biography*, 75

p.28: "My plans for the future are modest indeed . . ." *Madame Curie: A Biography*, 77

p.30: "And now you, my little Manya . . ." *Madame Curie: A Biography*, 83

p.31: "If you can't see a way to clear up . . . *Madame Curie: A Biography*, 88

p.34: "It's a foreigner with an impossible . . ." *Madame Curie: A Biography*, 95

p.34: "I take the sun and I throw it . . ." *Madame Curie: A Biography*, 97

p.34: "Don't trust what people teach you . . ." *Marie Curie: A Life* (Quinn), 99

p.35: "I shall always consider one of the best . . . ." *Pierre Curie*, 85

p.38: "all attempts to discover any effect of heat . . ." *Foundations of Modern Physical Science*, 337

For Further Study

This online summary of Marie Curie's contribution to science features a biography, quotes, and photographs: www.spaceandmotion.com/physics-marie-curie-biography.htm

The ChemSoc Timeline details important steps in the development of chemistry, including the contributions of important scientists: www.chemsoc.org/timeline/

Marie Curie's Nobel speech, which she gave in 1911, can be found here: gos.sbc.edu/c/curie1911.html

This kid-friendly site explains the science behind the spectral lines that come from glowing elements: www.colorado.edu/physics/2000/quantumzone/

Index

Acknowledgments

This book is dedicated to my cousin, Christine Guy Schnittka, a role model for female scientists and future science teachers. Additionally, I would like to thank Renaud Huynh, of the Marie Curie Museum in Paris, for his careful review of the manuscript.

Picture Credits

All the photographs in this book are used with permission and through the courtesy of:

Archives Curie et Joliot-Curie (ACJC): pp.1, 6, 9, 11, 12, 18, 19, 26, 29, 34, 56, 58, 65, 69, 70, 72, 76, 77, 81, 83, 93, 98, 101, 107, 111, 112, 118, 121, 122tr, 122bl, 123tc, 123br

American Institute of Physics (AIP): pp.48, 49, 63, 80, 87, 104, 119, 122tc, 123tl

Getty Images: pp.2–3, 23, 35, 73, 75, 86, 91, 123bl, Getty Images; 4–5, 16, 30, 55, 86, 89, 90, 100, 102 Roger Viollet; p.53 AFP; pp.60, 78, 85, 110, 124–125, 126–127 Popperfoto; p.61 Wilhelm Roentgen; p.94 Emmanuel Lansyer; p.97 Time and Life Pictures; p.116 Library of Congress

Alamy Images: pp.10, 122tl JTB Photo; p.15 Interfoto; pp.20, 33, 41, 59, 71, 84, 114 Mary Evans Picture Collection; p.21 Andrzej Gorzkowski; pp.24, 123tl Bildarchiv; p.25, 38, 43, 47, 50, 62, 67r, 96, 99, 105, 108, 113 The Print Collector; p.32 Pitu Cau; p.42 Phil Degginger; p.44 World History Archive; p.45 Phototake, Inc.; p.54 Tor Eigeland; p.68 Derrick Alderman; p.88 Visual Arts Library; p.106 Pictorial Press; p.120 Mediscan

Corbis: p.17 Hulton-Deutsch Collection; p.36 Burstein Collection; p.39 Alain Nogues; p.40 Bettman; p.79 Lester V. Bergman; pp.82, 122br Ted Spiegel; p.109 Visuals Unlimited

Excelsior: p.103 January 9, 1911

Dorling Kindersley: p.37 Mike Dunning; pp.46, 67l, 74 Clive Streeter; p.115 Gary Kevin

Bridgeman Art Library: pp.64, 122bc Institut de Radium; p.66 Archives Larousse; p.95 Private Collection

Library of Congress: pp.117, 123bc

BORDER PHOTOS, from left to right: ACJC; ACJC; Getty Images/William Roentgen; Excelsior; ACJC; ACJC; ACJC; ACJC; AIP; ACJC; ACJC; Getty Images/Roger Viollet; ACJC; AIP; AIP; Alamy Images/The Print Collector; ACJC

About the Author

Vicki Cobb worked as a laboratory researcher and science teacher before becoming a full-time writer. She is the author of more than 85 nonfiction books for children, including *DK Biography: Harry Houdini* and many hands-on science books. Passionate about education, she often gives science talks to teachers and students. Visit her at: www.vickicobb.com

Other DK Biographies you'll enjoy:

Charles Darwin
David C. King
ISBN 978-0-7566-2554-2 paperback
ISBN 978-0-7566-2555-9 hardcover

Princess Diana
Joanne Mattern
ISBN 978-0-7566-1614-4 paperback
ISBN 978-0-7566-1613-7 hardcover

Amelia Earhart
Tanya Lee Stone
ISBN 978-0-7566-2552-8 paperback
ISBN 978-0-7566-2553-5 hardcover

Albert Einstein
Frieda Wishinsky
ISBN 978-0-7566-1247-4 paperback
ISBN 978-0-7566-1248-1 hardcover

Benjamin Franklin
Stephen Krensky
ISBN 978-0-7566-3528-2 paperback
ISBN 978-0-7566-3529-9 hardcover

Gandhi
Amy Pastan
ISBN 978-0-7566-2111-7 paperback
ISBN 978-0-7566-2112-4 hardcover

Harry Houdini
Vicki Cobb
ISBN 978-0-7566-1245-0 paperback
ISBN 978-0-7566-1246-7 hardcover

Helen Keller
Leslie Garrett
ISBN 978-0-7566-0339-7 paperback
ISBN 978-0-7566-0488-2 hardcover

Joan of Arc
Kathleen Kudlinksi
ISBN 978-0-7566-3526-8 paperback
ISBN 978-0-7566-3527-5 hardcover

John F. Kennedy
Howard S. Kaplan
ISBN 978-0-7566-0340-3 paperback
ISBN 978-0-7566-0489-9 hardcover

Martin Luther King, Jr.
Amy Pastan
ISBN 978-0-7566-0342-7 paperback
ISBN 978-0-7566-0491-2 hardcover

Abraham Lincoln
Tanya Lee Stone
ISBN 978-0-7566-0834-7 paperback
ISBN 978-0-7566-0833-0 hardcover

Nelson Mandela
Lenny Hort & Laaren Brown
ISBN 978-0-7566-2109-4 paperback
ISBN 978-0-7566-2110-0 hardcover

Mother Teresa
Maya Gold
ISBN 978-0-7566-3880-1 paperback
ISBN 978-0-7566-3881-8 hardcover

Annie Oakley
Chuck Wills
ISBN 978-0-7566-2997-7 paperback
ISBN 978-0-7566-2986-1 hardcover

Pelé
Jim Buckley
ISBN 978-0-7566-2987-8 paperback
ISBN 978-0-7566-2996-0 hardcover

Eleanor Roosevelt
Kem Knapp Sawyer
ISBN 978-0-7566-1496-6 paperback
ISBN 978-0-7566-1495-9 hardcover

George Washington
Lenny Hort
ISBN 978-0-7566-0835-4 paperback
ISBN 978-0-7566-0832-3 hardcover

Look what the critics are saying about DK Biography!

"…highly readable, worthwhile overviews for young people…" —*Booklist*

"This new series from the inimitable DK Publishing brings together the usual brilliant photography with a historian's approach to biography subjects." —*Ingram Library Services*